Will Willimon

Heaven
and Earth

ADVENT *and the* INCARNATION

Abingdon Press | Nashville

Heaven and Earth
Advent and the Incarnation

Copyright © 2023 Abingdon Press
All rights reserved.

Library of Congress Control Number: 2023935972
978-1-7910-2903-6

MANUFACTURED IN THE
UNITED STATES OF AMERICA

CONTENTS

God Taking Time for Us

Happy New Year!

That's right. It's Advent, the Christian New Year.

As the world's year ends, the Christian year begins. In December, the world wearily plods toward the termination of another year. Days grow shorter, nights get longer. Welcome 2024! Sounds as exciting as Welcome 2014, or 2004. One year comes, another goes. What's changed? Who cares? We're still stuck with things as they are, which too closely resemble things as they always have been. There is nothing new under the sun (Ecclesiastes 1:9). Not much new to toast in the new year. Congratulations. You are one year older! Rejoice!

No wonder that New Year's Eve parties are known for overconsumption of alcohol. Unhappy New Year. Take a sledgehammer to your brain so you won't think about the beginning of yet another year.

Why make New Year's resolutions? Our resolve won't last past Super Bowl Sunday. We'd like to put aside old behaviors and take up new, healthy habits, to make the new year a time for fresh beginnings. Still, we suspect there's a good chance that the new year will resemble the old. Same old you. Tiresome old me. Stuck.

Then the church gives us Advent, the beginning of the Church Year, four weeks to take time, mark time, and make time differently from the way the world keeps time. The appointed Advent scriptures are an answer to a number of New Year's questions: Are we ending or beginning? Are our human efforts the only agency in history? Have we come to the end of the road, or is something new afoot? Is it the same old thing, or a fresh start? Are we stuck, abandoned to our own devices? Or is it possible that God might show up and disrupt, intervene, shake up, and take time for us?

It's not within our own power to make a fresh start. If we're to have a future different from the past, it must come as a gift, something not of our devising. What we need is a God who refuses to be trapped in eternity, a Creator who is not aloof from our time. We need a God who not only cares about us but who is willing to show up among us and do something with us, here, now.

Good news! Advent, marking the church's New Year, says, in a number of different ways, that's just the sort of God we've got.

Reflecting on some of the Gospel readings appointed for Advent, let's take time to meditate upon the God who has, in the advent of the Babe of Bethlehem, Mighty Savior, Light of the World, taken time for us. Jesus's name means "God saves," which is a Bible way of saying that Almighty God has turned toward us. God is not confined in heaven. God stoops toward us, intervening, showing up when least expected and in ways that surprise. All in God's good time. Advent is God taking time *from* us by making time *for* us.

It's Advent. You've got four weeks to adjust to the jolt of God taking time for us. So brace yourself to welcome the God you didn't expect, the God who climbs down to us because we couldn't climb up to God. Ready or not, God is on the way.

Will Willimon

Chapter

1

Meanwhile

CHAPTER 1

Meanwhile

"In those days, after the suffering of that time, the sun will become dark, and the moon won't give its light. The stars will fall from the sky, and the planets and other heavenly bodies will be shaken. Then they will see the Human One coming in the clouds with great power and splendor. Then he will send the angels and gather together his chosen people from the four corners of the earth, from the end of the earth to the end of heaven....

"But nobody knows when that day or hour will come, not the angels in heaven and not the Son. Only the Father knows. Watch out! Stay alert! You don't know when the time is coming. It is as if someone took a trip, left the household behind, and put the servants in charge, giving each one a job to do, and told the doorkeeper to stay alert. Therefore, stay alert! You don't know when the head of the household will come, whether in the evening or at midnight, or when the rooster crows in the early

morning or at daybreak. Don't let him show up when
you weren't expecting and find you sleeping. What I say
to you, I say to all: Stay alert!"

(Mark 13:24-27, 32-37)

Jesus—on the way out of the temple on that last visit—takes time to predict that in a short while the beloved, magnificent temple will be utterly destroyed (Mark 13:2). In Jesus's longest sermon in Mark's Gospel, Jesus rants that not one stone will be left on another. Imagine the shock among the faithful when they heard Jesus speak of the destruction of the building that was built to look eternal. The grand temple, meant to appear as if it had always been here and always would be, according to Jesus would very soon cease to exist.

More bad news. Jesus expands the apocalyptic (apocalypse = revelation), earth-shattering predictions beyond the temple:

In those days, after the suffering of that time, the sun will
become dark, and the moon won't give its light. The stars
will fall from the sky, and the planets and other heavenly
bodies will be shaken.

(Mark 13:24-25)

Advent begins with apocalyptic talk of the world's end. Our cherished religious institutions, beautiful creations, and time-honored traditions will "in those days," in "that time" be dismantled, the whole cosmos shaken. Stars and planets, so reassuring in their constant courses, will be dislodged, turned upside down, deconstructed, all shook up.

My Lord, what a morning, when the stars begin to fall.

(African American spiritual)

We claimed that we wanted Advent, said that we yearned for God to come to us. We prayed that God would descend from heaven to us.

But when God took us seriously and actually came down among us, God's Advent was so earthshaking that many ran for cover. Trouble is, we wanted God on our terms, not God's. We wanted God quietly and gently to slip in beside us, not kick in the door, blow the house down, tear up our temples, and shake us up.

The prophet Isaiah pled, during one of the many difficult days in Israel's history, "If only you would tear open the heavens and come down!" (Isaiah 64:1). But Jesus speaks of God's coming as an event that tears up not just heaven, but the whole world. Be careful what you pray for.

SHAKEN

Most of us have been conditioned to think that church is personal. Just Jesus and me. So much of our praise music is packed with first-person pronouns. I. Me. My. Mine. Religion is a private matter, something just between the two of us. Church is where we go, if we go, to have some personal time with a God who sometimes gives us assistance with our individual problems.

"What does that have to do with me?" is the question that's put to every sermon. "What's in it for me?"

Therefore it's a jolt to be told, on the First Sunday of Advent, that when God at last turns toward us, God is about more than mere healing, moral renovation, or a helpful spiritual nudge for individuals. God's intentions are no less than cosmic: heaven and earth shaken, darkened sun and moon and stars falling from the sky.

God is about more than mere healing, moral renovation, or a helpful spiritual nudge for individuals. God's intentions are no less than cosmic: heaven and earth shaken, darkened sun and moon and stars falling from the sky.

Powerful, privileged people (like most of us North American mainline Christians) get nervous when the talk turns edgy apocalyptic. Such highly charged, poetic language sounds unsophisticated, primitive, even fundamentalist. What would my sophisticated friends, who already think this church stuff is whacko, think of me if they heard Jesus on the world's end? And after all, down through the ages, those Christians who took Jesus's predictions literally, thinking that they had come up with a date for the end of the world, have always been wrong. Right?

Don't flatter yourself that you are put off by Jesus's apocalyptic predictions because you are so sophisticated, modern, and urbane. People on top, well-fed and happily ensconced, tend always to believe that this world is as good as it gets. Don't pray for change; work the world as it is to your advantage and privilege. Church is where we come to nail things down. The Christian faith is a primitive technique for holding on to what you've got. Stop whining about your troubles in the present; cease dreaming about the future. Adjust. This is as good as it gets. The best of times. Learn to be happy with things as they are. Steady, upward progress is easier on the psyche than abrupt death of the old and birth of the new.

So the church plods along as always, for two thousand years brushing off Jesus's talk of the sky falling and the sun being extinguished, reassuring ourselves. Relax. Jesus doesn't know what he's talking about. Didn't happen then and won't happen now.

Jesus, keep your disruptive, earthshaking apocalyptic visions to yourself.

Then came COVID-19, the nightmarish body counts on the nightly news, impotent old men refusing to vacate high places, trouble in the streets, broken glass, conspiracy theories, revolutionary rumblings among the young, dire predictions by Fox News, fear on the right and the left. Get yourself a gun. Cower behind locked doors. The penny dropped. Jesus's apocalyptic prophecies about the end began to make sense.

When things are going well for me personally—my children are well fed and my days are reasonably sunny; I'm secure in my gated community, clutching my 401(k) to my heart, eating organic, and working out at the gym now and then—I'm not too concerned about others whose needs are greater than mine.

I take out an insurance policy, purchase an alarm system, and hold on to what I've got even more tightly. It's disconcerting to have Jesus say to us, as Advent begins, that this world (that we've worked reasonably well to our advantage) is terminal. It's scary to hear Jesus announce that we are profoundly unsafe.

Texts like Mark 13 explain why most of our churches bolt the pews to the floor, the furnishings are heavier than they need to be, and the building is made to look five hundred years older than it really is. This is church twisted into a means of keeping our world safe from the cosmic shakings of Jesus. Plodding through the order of worship, seated row upon row in our fixed-in-place pews, singing familiar hymns in unison without missing a beat, huddled with folks like us, beginning and ending right on time, secures us from the possibility of a God who just can't leave us be.

"Lord, we didn't mean what we said when we asked you to come down and save us. Just give us some helpful guidance whereby we might be improved rather than saved. Better still, why don't you just leave well enough alone?"

Advent scripture says that our stratagems for being left alone won't work because of who God is and what God is up to.

First, God is relentless—fecund Creator who didn't just begin the world and then retire. God keeps working with the world, bringing something out of nothing, light out of darkness, and form out of chaos, birthing a new you out of the old. There are many millennia of our well-documented human screwups, and still God's not done with us yet.

God keeps working with the world, bringing something out of nothing, light out of darkness, and form out of chaos, birthing a new you out of the old.

Second, God is love. Love's not love that abandons the beloved. There's much that we don't know about God, but this we know for sure from reading nearly any verse of scripture: God is determined to find a way to love us, to converse with us, to fulfill God's promises to us, even if God's got to rock our world in order to get the love that God wants.

Should the true and living God be turning toward us, there are bound to be jolts and bumps, some shaking along the way. Something must die in order for anything to be born. The first name for Christians was the Way (Acts 9; 19; 22)—people on the way toward God, or God making a way toward us, take it either way. We're not where God wants us to be, not by a long shot. "We don't have a permanent city here, but rather we are looking for the city that is still to come" (Hebrews 13:14). If we're going to follow Jesus, we must learn to sit lightly on present arrangements.

Standing on the sidewalk before a storefront ministry for and with the homeless that she had managed for two decades, I asked the manager, "How have you been able to keep at such demanding ministry for so long?"

She waved her hand over the gray ruin that was that part of the city and said, "Scripture keeps reminding me that all of this is temporary. God refuses to let what we've made of this town be eternal. Bad news for the guys who own those buildings and run the city; good news for folks who sleep on the streets."

What can we expect of God? A homeowner sleeps, secure in his stuff (Matthew 24:43, read the First Sunday of Advent, Year A). During the night, the proprietor awakes. A thief has kicked in his door, invaded his cozy alliance with the status quo, broken in and ripped off everything. Jesus warns us to live as if all we think is ours, safe and sound, is about to be ripped off. Losers, watch out, wake up!

God the Thief, the Great Rip Off, not the most flattering divine image, to be sure. Good news or bad? Much depends on how tightly you're holding on to your stuff when you receive the news.

Jesus apocalyptically strides out of the temple and into the world, letting the disciples in on an open secret: *God is launching a great invasion to take back what belongs to God.* A new world breaking into the old. A whole lot of shakin' going on.

Spoiler alert: A few days after this announcement of the end of the temple in Mark 13, Jesus shook even the tight grip of death. In Jesus's cross and resurrection, Jesus didn't just come back from the dead, he also turned time on its head. Which is probably why Matthew (27:51-52) says that when Jesus on the cross breathed his last breath, rocks split, the earth heaved, and tombs were broken open. Three days later, when Jesus walked forth from the tomb, the earth violently shook and the stone rolled away. Jesus, in his death and in his resurrection, an earthquake.

Or, as Paul said, trying his best to explain the Resurrection to thickheaded King Agrippa (Acts 26:26), "This didn't happen secretly or in some out-of-the-way place." This thing—the birth, crucifixion, and resurrection of Jesus—is cosmic, world-shaking, time-disrupting. God won't be tucked away in your heart, or confined to an hour at church on Sunday morning, or limited to matters personal and private. God thinks God owns it all and God is going to get back what belongs to God.

Apocalyptic Jesus refuses to allow God to be used as the cement of social conformity or to have the gospel trimmed down to common sense. Buttoned-down, mainline Christianity has always been nervous about Jesus's apocalyptic talk. Those of us who have successfully scrambled our way to the top find the gospel easier to manage when it's toned down to soothe the anxious consciences of those of us who benefit from things as they are. But to people on the bottom or at the margins, all who are paralyzed and hopeless from fear, oppressed by the system, trapped in inescapable prisons, Jesus's apocalyptic is good news. Help is on the way. God is taking time for us.

Apocalyptic is good news because it's not simply about ending; it's also beginning. Jesus speaks of dismantling and deconstruction to alert us to the birth of something new. God's creativity doesn't end at Genesis; dismantling and disruption presage New Creation.

The psalmist sings,

God is our refuge and strength,
   a help always near in times of great trouble.
That's why we won't be afraid when the world falls apart,
      when the mountains crumble into the center of the sea,
      when its waters roar and rage,
      when the mountains shake because of its surging waves....

Come, see the LORD's *deeds,*
      what devastation he has imposed on the earth—
      bringing wars to an end in every corner of the world,
      breaking the bow and shattering the spear,
          burning chariots with fire.

                              (Psalm 46:1-3, 8-9)

"Times of great trouble" can be, in God's hand, seasons of deliverance, though there may be some "devastation" and "shattering" in the meanwhile. Bad news for those who've trusted in the bow, spear, and chariot; good news for those who've got no refuge and strength except God.

The Lord is busy. "Times of great trouble" can be, in God's hand, seasons of deliverance, though there may be some "devastation" and "shattering" in the meanwhile. Bad news for those who've trusted in the bow, spear, and chariot; good news for those who've got no refuge and strength except God.

We preachers tend to value stability, continuity, order, and placidity in our congregations. We worry about those who are discontent with things as they are, troublemakers who speak out and act up, grumblers who are unhappy with the church's status quo.

We ought to be more worried about all those who are just bored to death, those who don't walk out of church in a huff but quietly quit attending because they've given up on anything new happening, anything disconcerting being said. For these malcontents, a church rumble now and then would be a welcomed sign of life.

So here comes Jesus in Mark 13 speaking of heavens broken open, quotidian cycles ended, the earth convulsing, and the whole creation heaving. "Jesus, give us a word of hope before you go." Mark 13 is the word Jesus spoke, wanted or not.

We liked it when Jesus urged us to love one another, to welcome the little children, consider the lilies, offer a cup of water. But when Jesus goes apocalyptic, well. . . .

A billboard outside of town proclaims "The Bible Has the Answer to All Your Questions, It's the Key to All Your Problems." Really? I know people who could say that they didn't have tough problems or perplexing questions until they started reading the

Bible. Much depends on what you define as your problems and what you would accept as solutions.

Yet, be honest now, is there not something within you that yearns to be all shook up?

"I like Joe," a man said of his preacher, "but he's no great preacher. Hard to follow. And our choir? It never was much; but, after the pandemic, our choir is nothing but a few aging sopranos and one rickety, former tenor."

I asked the obvious question. "Why do you still hang in there?"

He responded, "I'm still attending that church because a few years ago, one Sunday, as the sermon was ending, just before the last hymn, it was like God grabbed me by the scruff of the neck, shook me up and down, took hold of me, and changed my world forever. God hasn't repeated that in years. But God could. That's why I show up on Sunday, hoping that God might light that fire again."

HERE COMES GOD

Then they will see the Human One coming in the clouds with great power and splendor. Then he will send the angels and gather together his chosen people from the four corners of the earth, from the end of the earth to the end of heaven.

(Mark 13:26–27)

On most days, the majority of people in my church can solve most of our problems and meet most of our challenges on our own. Sure, we've got our issues, but just get the right people in government, or find the wise counsel from some guru, come up with a workable solution to what ails us, and we can save ourselves by ourselves. Pity those who have fewer resources, or less freedom, or too little money. But maybe, with hard work, grit, and ambition, they can be just as self-sufficiently godless as the rest of us.

While channel surfing one Sunday, I dropped in briefly on sermons in four churches. Here's a one-sentence summary of each: (1) What you don't know about personal trauma can kill you. Here's what you need to think about when the world has been bad to you. (2) There's enough for everybody if we just had better logistics. Shame on you if you're not working for better food distribution. (3) If you aren't voting for control of guns, particularly automatic weapons, you are part of the problem. Don't you want to be the solution? (4) We have got to step up and stand up to the radical gay agenda. There's nothing more important than getting godly (i.e., Republican) men (and I mean men) on the Supreme Court.

Notice anything missing in those sermons? *God.*

Church is where we come to be reminded of our responsibilities, to listen to our better angels, to step up and do something about our problems. It's all about us.

Thus we show up on Sunday to receive our to-do list for the week: "Here are all the things wrong with the world today. Come back next week and I'll give you another list. It's up to us to set the world right or right won't be done. Stop wasting time asking God to come to your aid. Get busy!"

Or else the sermon is where we are given tips for self-improvement: "Here are four biblical principles that, if you follow them, will give you a happy marriage." Or "Want to feel better about yourself? Diets, cosmetics, and workouts can only take you so far. While the Bible could not care less about most of your contemporary fixations, as a preacher, I'm an expert on human relations so let me tell you what you can do to have a more positive self-image. Write this down!" Who needs God to help you be the you that you want you to be?

Maybe we limit Christian concerns to the personal, individual, and private because, not knowing how to fix the world, we try to modify ourselves, which, you know if you've ever tried to do something to change yourself by yourself, is absurd. Still, we try.

God's up there in heaven; we're down here on earth. Maybe there was a day when we could expect divine intervention, but that was a long time ago. We couldn't get the modern world going without first securing ourselves safe from God's agency. Beginning in the seventeenth century, we attempted to make a world in which God wasn't needed and didn't matter, a clockwork cosmos protected from divine incursions. God, stay up there so we can be free to handle things as we darn well please down here. If we can just research, develop, and organize, we can control the world. Though we can't (yet) control the weather, we can at least predict it. Given enough time and government funding, maybe we can control that too.

Look at us, we've got the whole world in our hands.

We can't have God showing up and disrupting our wonderfully well-functioning, modern machine of a world. Back in Bible times (Mark 13) people needed God to do for them some of the many things they were powerless to control. Not us. We don't pray to end a pandemic; we develop the drugs to stop the virus. We don't ask God to stop Putin's aggression, we send in the drones. We can do anything we put our minds to. I don't beg God to give me a more positive attitude toward life; I take a pill. Look at us.

Sure, there are still problems. Our vaunted human development also destroyed the environment. Some of our wars on disease created new diseases. Occasionally we had to destroy a town in order to save it. Now and then, things didn't turn out as we had planned. If Putin would only behave. If people would just wash their hands and eat organic. Still, there's only us to save the world or the world won't be saved. God is up there and we are down here. Roll up your sleeves, get organized, get busy.

If things are set right between us and God, God's got to do it.

Then comes the First Sunday of Advent and Jesus insists on talking about God rather than us. Behind this strange, interventionist, apocalyptic talk is a countercultural claim: If things are set right between us and God, God's got to do it. The same Creator who lovingly created the world must keep creating, keep overcoming the darkness with light, continue

17

to push back the threatening chaos bringing something out of nothing or we are utterly without hope.

"How did you get into church planting?" I asked the young pastor. There we stood, in a once-abandoned, now renovated, former crack house that was now aptly named Church of the Second Chance.

"In my last church, I grew so tired of the triviality of it all, the pettiness," he explained. "We weren't much more than a friendly, congenial club of like-minded, middle-class folks. I wanted to try something so big, so out-of-the-box that if God wasn't in it, if God refused to bless it, we'd fall flat on our faces. Turns out, we have a more resourceful God than I dared to imagine."

The deistic God of the philosophers, a minimalist, inactive, unobtrusive, noninvasive, unrevealing God is about as much of God as we moderns can take. Jesus the teacher of morality, a really nice person who loved lilies and was kind to children and people with disabilities; Jesus the all-affirming, never-judging friend who always tells you what you want to hear.

No, says apocalyptic Jesus. This Jesus, named God Saves, is a peripatetic, wild Jew from Nazareth who won't stay confined within our boundaries for God. He comes to cast fire on the earth, tear apart families (Matthew 10:35), topple kingdoms, and thereby offer us a refashioned world we could never create by ourselves.

Apocalyptic Advent accuses us not of having asked too much of God, but rather of having settled for too little. Many of our congregations have limited themselves to that which human effort alone can accomplish and trimmed down our prayers to the purely personal. "God, here are a few things, mostly related to my health, that I need help with in the coming week," rather than daring to pray as Jesus taught us, "Bring in your kingdom so that your will is done on earth as it's done in heaven." Bring it on, Lord!

I came across a sermon by a preacher from Houston who preaches to more people than have ever listened to my sermons. I won't use his name. That would be unprofessional. His sermon was titled "How to Get Close to Heaven" or "What You Need to Do to Get Noticed" or "Hey, We're Down Here Pedaling as Fast as We Can." Something like that. The preacher said that you can't just show up at church. You've got to prepare yourself. Put yourself into the right frame of mind. Cultivate a teachable spirit. Stop taking potshots at the preacher. Forgive the off-key choir. On Saturday, ask yourself, "What do I need most in my life?" "Which problems do I need fixed?"

(I muttered to myself, "Lots of luck, Joel. It's all I can do just to get my folks to show up on Sundays. They're not going to do homework!")

Notice anything missing from the preacher's sermon (and my response)? *God.*

On the First Sunday of Advent, Mark 13 and Jesus insist that we talk about God rather than ourselves. Our Deistic, detached, alleged-to-be-loving-but-mostly-inactive deities are exposed for what they are: a vain, modern attempt to protect ourselves from the intrusions and judgments of a living, active, real God.

"You better try hard to believe that God is still active in creation," said the noted Christian environmentalist at the Saving the Earth conference. "Set out to end global warming or make a significant impact on carbon emissions, it won't be long until you see the futility of your efforts. Recycling your bottles and cans won't get you to your goal. Despair sets in. You'll give up. You must believe that God loves the world and is still caring for the world in order for you to keep working for the world. You've got to know that you work with the grain of the universe, that your efforts to clean up the mess we've made are not the only thing that's going on, or you'll quit."

Fred Craddock told of a young preacher who made a reluctant pastoral visit to an older member of his congregation who was in the hospital in the last days of her life. He entered the sick room and there she lay, her head back on the pillow. He could hear her gasping for breath.

He resolved not to sap her strength with a long visit. After initial pleasantries, he asked, "Why don't we pray? What would you like me to pray for?"

Between her wheezes she said, "That...I'll...be healed, of course."

He sighed. Then he prayed something like, "Lord, if it be thy will, please deliver this sister from her illness and pain. But if it is not thy will, we pray that you would be with her, that you would help her to better accept her situation, however this turns out, etc. Amen."

The moment he ended his prayer, the woman's eyes opened. She lifted her head, then she sat up. She threw her feet over the side of the bed. "I think I'm healed," she exclaimed before a dumbfounded pastor. "Yes. I feel strong. I'm healed!"

The young man stood stupefied as he watched her get up and trot down to the nurses' station, proclaiming, "I'm healed!"

The pastor left the room and staggered down the hospital steps without a word. When he got back to his preachermobile, he put his hand upon the door, looked up to heaven and shouted, *"Don't you ever do that to me again!"*

How many Christians are languishing in the pews, quietly hoping, praying that even in their aggressively bright, cheerful, upbeat churches a few stars may fall, their souls shaken, and they be given some new beginning with God?

How many Christians are languishing in the pews, quietly hoping, praying that even in their aggressively bright, cheerful, upbeat churches a few stars may fall, their souls shaken, and they be given some new beginning with God?

Funny how the Christmases past that I most vividly remember were those when there was some unexpected disruption of our plans—the Christmas Eve blizzard when we took in a stranded traveler; the year that my uncle, on his way to see us, had to be hospitalized; the Christmas when I had to bang on my neighbor's door in the middle of the night and ask for help putting together the gym set for the kids.

A while back an Anglican priest came to see me. He had read some of my work and said he wanted to tell me about his momentous move. (We lowly Methodists love it when Anglicans ask us for advice.) He told me a story I've heard from others: beginning ministry with enthusiasm and spirit, then gradually suffocating in the muck and mire of the trivialities of congregational life; becoming bored, stalled; and now having decided to leave parish ministry.

"I'm telling them Wednesday night at the vestry. And no amount of begging is going to get me to stay," he said.

We had prayer and then I sent him on his way, asking him to keep me posted. A few weeks later I realized I hadn't heard from the poor man. I called him.

"Oh that," he replied. "I'm still here, happily," he said.

"Really? You're staying? Why?"

"Well, we went through the agenda for the vestry meeting. Then I said, 'I have an announcement. I'm leaving the ministry.' Tears and gasps. 'I used to love being a priest but we just spent an hour debating the repaving of the church parking lot! I loved ministry, but this is not what I was called to do. I'm out.'"

Then he said the oldest member of the vestry, a septuagenarian in a pink pantsuit, said, "You mean there is something that you felt God was calling you to say or to do that you haven't said or done because of us? We're holding you back from creative, courageous ministry? I think I've heard all your sermons this past year and I don't recall anything that suggested you were unhappy with the things as they are around here. Let me get this straight, we are keeping you from doing what God is calling you to do?"

He said he gulped and replied, "Well, we'd have to take a hard look at who we are and what we're doing. Admit the time we waste in pointlessness. We'd need to recruit some new leadership. Take a look at our congregation and who's not here and how God might help us to reach them."

"'Go ahead,' she said. 'Anybody here opposed to that?'"

"We had the first honest conversation in my four years at that church. There were tears, truth, a spirit not of our devising, and sometime just before eleven that night, even though we're Anglicans, we got born again."

How many congregations are stuck in the mire of the mundane, boring themselves to tears, awaiting God to give them the life-giving, heavenly jolt that could give them a future?

WHEN?

From the first, it's never been enough for some to hear Jesus say that God is coming to shake things up; they've demanded to know, *when?*

Jesus is not clear about exactly what will happen in that earthshaking, star-falling Advent of the Lord. But he is definite that the timing is not up to us (Mark 13:32-37). Even though Jesus warned us against speculation on a time line for God's promised apocalypse, down through the years, many have been disappointed that God doesn't work on our schedule.

From what I've seen as a pastor, waiting for God to show up is one of the most challenging aspects of staying in love with God. Lots of Christians may believe in an interventionist, intrusive, active God, yet their problem is that God takes God's own sweet time to do so. They know that God loves and cares, but what they need, in the worst sort of way, is for God to love and care for them *now*.

The cancer that won't go away. The divided family that refuses reunion. The church that can't scrape up the funds to live another year. The war that won't end. The wound that doesn't heal. Where is God, *now*?

I know somebody who sincerely believes that Jesus wants her to forgive someone who has committed a terrible wrong against her. Her assailant has repented and sincerely begged for her forgiveness.

"I've prayed every day for the past ten years for Jesus to come and help me do what he wants me to do, but Jesus hasn't," she told me.

Mark's constant stress on the cross-bearing and suffering of disciples suggests that this gospel hoped to strengthen early Christians as they bore the slings and arrows of a disbelieving world. A subtext of Mark 13 is thus, "hold on, be resilient, stay strong because Christ's Second Advent is on the way! He will rescue, save, and preserve you. Keep the faith!"

Their chief question: *when?*

"God is good, all the time. All the time, God is good," you sometimes hear said in worship. If that's true, what's keeping God from being more active in my time, our time, now?

Therefore a cardinal Advent virtue is patience, the faithful willingness to wait, to not have God on demand, to allow God to come and to go as God pleases, to let Christ enter our time in Christ's own good time. Besides, grace (meaning, "gift") is not grace if it's at our command.

Why is God taking so long to fulfill the cosmic, heaven-and-earth–shaking promises of Mark 13? Maybe God takes God's time in order to give us more time. By not shaking the heavens a few decades after the death and resurrection of Jesus (when we think Mark was written), we are given more time to come to terms with Jesus and to allow Jesus to come to terms with us.

Jesus commanded his followers, us, to go into all the world, teaching and baptizing all nations (Matthew 28), to be shining lights in the world, demonstrating to the world what God can do when ordinary people obey Jesus (Matthew 5), showing everybody, everywhere the truth about God (Acts 1:8). We've needed more than two thousand years to be obedient and are still not there yet. Thanks be to God, there's still time.

What if God had pulled the plug two thousand years ago? No Mother Teresa, no Martin Luther King Jr., no Saint Francis of Assisi, no Bono, no you or me. You may not be the finest disciple there ever was, but because the predictions of Mark 13 didn't come to immediate fulfillment, there's still time. God isn't done with you yet.

Jesus predicts, *Then he will send the angels and gather together his chosen people from the four corners of the earth, from the end of the earth to the end of heaven* (Mark 13:27). There's still time for fractured, divided people of God—scattered to the four corners

25

of the earth, bickering with one another, divided by their differences—to be brought together, convened, congregated by the Human One.

I've worked for the healing of divisions in my denomination, saying and doing what I can to get us on the same page, to keep folks from walking out. I'm glad to hear Mark say that Christ is taking the time to reunite us, regathering *his chosen people from the four corners of the earth*. Looks like that promised reunion may happen after I'm gone. Still, I'm glad that Christ is taking all the time we need to do what he expects us to do, even if my time may be up before it's done.

In delaying the end, perhaps God is not only teaching us patience but also showing us what true patience looks like. In the meanwhile, God not only takes time out of our hands but God also makes time for us. Patiently working with fractured, disobedient humanity down through the ages, God showed amazing forbearance, tolerance, and unflappable perseverance. As soon as we were given the Ten Commandments, we broke them. Prophets came and went and we failed to heed their words. We were offered God's own Son; we crucified Jesus. Mark took the time to write his Gospel for us; we explained it away, dismissing its sermons as woefully out of date.

Yet even when we nailed the Son of God to a cross, this long-suffering, patient God looks down upon us wasting our time and says, "I love you still. In the meanwhile, there's yet time for you to learn to love the God who so eternally loves you."

WHAT NOW?

So what do we do in the meanwhile? That's a good Advent question. When it was my turn to have COVID-19, thank God I had a mild case. Still, bedridden with a fever, those few days seemed like an eternity. The worst part was the waiting. At times I felt very sick, but not so sick that I didn't want to be up and out in the world. Life passed me by. There are too many hours in a day when one spends them in bed. I wanted to be well, to be up and at 'em, and I wanted that *now*.

After recovering, as I was grousing to a friend about how miserable I had felt, my friend surprised me by asking, "What did your illness teach you? What did you learn about yourself and God while you were bedridden?"

What? My illness is supposed to be a learning experience? What? Killing time sick in bed can be redemptive if it's true all my time is still God's time?

> *"But nobody knows when that day or hour will come, not the angels in heaven and not the Son. Only the Father knows. Watch out! Stay alert! You don't know when the time is coming. It is as if someone took a trip, left the household behind, and put the servants in charge, giving each one a job to do, and told the doorkeeper to stay alert. Therefore, stay alert! You don't know when the head of the household will come, whether in the evening or at midnight, or when the rooster crows in the early morning or at daybreak. Don't let him show up when you weren't expecting and find you sleeping. What I say to you, I say to all: Stay alert!"*

When? Nobody knows (Mark 13:32). But just because nobody knows, that's no reason to put the end out of our minds. Just the reverse. Three times Jesus repeats his admonition, "Stay alert!" (vv. 33, 35, 37).

Mark's Gospel recorded these words less than a hundred years after Jesus spoke them. That's a long time to stay awake. Early Christians believed that the time would be short between Christ's first Advent and his next. Eager expectancy is a hard emotion to maintain over the long run. Yet Jesus commands his followers to stay awake.

We pray the Advent prayer, "Come, Lord Jesus!" at the end of the Bible and the beginning of the church (Revelation 22:20). That's the church's earnest desire, "Thy kingdom come, thy will be done. God, show yourself to us. Come on down, Holy Spirit. Maranatha! Come, Lord Jesus!"

Still, we wait. The cancer will not heal. Sure faith doesn't come. There is no peace. Creation continues to be imperiled. We wait. The prophet's prayer that God would "tear open the heavens and come down" (Isaiah 64:1) is unfulfilled. We wait.

Yet in the meanwhile we don't have to wait with nothing to do. I know a medical researcher who has been patiently, but not passively, waiting to discover a drug that will knock out a particular kind of rare but deadly disease. Her wait consists of five days a week, nine hours a day in the lab or poring over research data, trying this, venturing that, daily conversing and sharing results with dozens of fellow scientists. She's waiting for the discovery that solves the problem, but she's not doing nothing while she waits.

Mark 13 urges that sort of waiting.

Watch out! Stay alert! You don't know when the time is coming.

"We can solve the hunger problem in Trenton," a congregation said to itself. A plan was devised whereby each Sunday, a basket was placed in front of the Lord's Table. During the Communion, people would bring canned goods, packages of food, disposable diapers, toiletry items, bread, and place them in the basket.

The first week, ten people received the free food. Next week, twenty showed up. The Food Committee urged congregants to be even more generous, since the need was greater than they first thought. By the third Monday, thirty people were standing in line at the church. The food gave out after the first twenty.

Gradually it dawned on the congregation that they were not going to solve the hunger problem in Trenton. Enthusiasm for the project waned. Their basket, filled to the brim every week, would never be an adequate response to the need. They lobbied the city council for help with food deprivation in the city. Some aid was given. But not enough.

"It's a waste of time," some in the congregation scoffed. "Not a practical, effective long-term solution," others said.

One of the youngest members spoke up. "No, it's what Jesus wants. I don't know how to solve the problem of hunger in Trenton. But I do know that Jesus expects me to notice, to pray, then to respond to the best of my ability. At times I feel overwhelmed, depressed by the needs I see in this town, right around our church. Maybe only God can finally solve this. But in the meanwhile, I do what I can.

"Besides," she added, "the Sunday food basket is the first time in a long time that our church has done much of anything for our neighborhood. That food basket may be doing this church more good than it's helping folks in need. Maybe we're the ones in need—in need of doing something for Jesus."

Mark 13 urges that sort of waiting. Advent is about that sort of waiting.

We can't bring the history of the world to successful conclusion. We, by our meager efforts, cannot fulfill all of God's intentions for God's Creation. We wait and work and pray ("Come, Lord!" 1 Corinthians 16:22) for the consummation that is only God's to give.

In the meantime, we do what we can, letting our little light shine, enabling people to see our good works, meager though they may be in the larger scheme of things, as signs, signals, and portents of the great good work Jesus promises to do in the end. Our job, in the meantime, is to tell and to show that Christ has come and will come again, to let the world in on the open secret that God isn't done with us yet. Christ, the light of the world, has commissioned us to be his lights in the world. As Mark 13:10 says, this time between Advents is time for mission, witness, testimony, and evangelism. Before the grand Second Advent consummation, *First, the good news must be proclaimed to all the nations.*

At the end of my visit with a young man incarcerated in our local jail, he said, speaking from behind iron bars, "Thanks for taking the time to come see me. Sitting here in this godforsaken cage, I had almost forgot. God will make a way. It ain't over for me till God says it's over. God's got the time even while I'm doin' time."

By the grace of God, there's still time for the good news to be proclaimed and enacted in your neighborhood and mine.

> *You don't know when the time is coming. It is as if someone took a trip, left the household behind, and put the servants in charge, giving each one a job to do, and told the doorkeeper to stay alert. Therefore, stay alert!*

In the meantime, between Christ's first Advent and the Second, Christ has done the usual vocational thing: *put the servants in charge, giving each one a job to do.* We, somnambulant, inadequate servants though we are, having been given a portion of Christ's realm to share with the world, have the time to be faithful.

I once served a dwindling, inner-city congregation. Once, we were a lively young church in a burgeoning new neighborhood on the edge of town. By the time I got there we had aged into a small, struggling congregation where most of our members commuted from other parts of the city. What could we do to have a future?

During a Bible study session one night, one of the members said something to the effect of "it's sad that we live in a time when so many young parents are having babies, starting families, without family nearby. They're stuck in these young-adult apartments with people their age who know as little about raising babies as they. Nobody to help, no adoring grandparents around."

Somehow the Holy Spirit must have shown up and insinuated itself into the conversation because, before the evening ended, we were on our way to devising the "Northside Baby Welcome."

We selected a set of stereotypical grandparents and commissioned them to visit every baby born on our turf. By checking the newborn list at the local hospital, it was easy to find where new babies lived. About a week after the baby was brought to a home in our neighborhood, our official "Baby Visitors" showed up on the parents' doorstep asking, "Can we see our new neighbor?"

The generic grandparents bore a children's Bible storybook ("Never too soon to start reading to the baby," the parents were told), a pamphlet on baby care, and a set of disposable diapers. The visitors said, "Our church is right down the street. Children are our top priority. When you visit, you'll find a group of talented, vetted caregivers to greet you. We also have a new Parents Morning Out program. First two visits free. Children's bulletins for worship too. Just want you to know that you don't have to be parents alone. We're here to help."

For the first time in a decade, there was growth. God took that Baby Welcome program and made it a successful evangelistic opportunity. Yet what I remember most was the comment, made sometime during Advent as I recall, "You know, this church has never really had a mission, never really connected with our own neighborhood. We built these buildings and Sunday school rooms thirty years ago, mostly for our own kids. Now, God has at last given us a purpose. We have a mission to our time and place. It took us three decades to discover it. Glad that the Lord gave us the time to figure it out and get in gear with God."

Maybe, since Jesus's advent, any time God turns to us and we see ending and beginning, it's apocalypse. In Jesus's first Advent, Jesus had a habit of showing up when people weren't expecting him, inviting himself into their lives, going where he wasn't even wanted.

> It is as if someone took a trip, left the household behind, and put the servants in charge, giving each one a job to do, and told the doorkeeper to stay alert. Therefore, stay alert! You don't know when the head of the household will come, whether in the evening or at midnight, or when the rooster crows in the early morning or at daybreak. Don't let him show up when you weren't expecting and find you sleeping. What I say to you, I say to all: Stay alert!

What do we do between Advents? We live as if God were to show up among us right now, at any time, day or night at any place, here or there. We are to keep alert, stay awake, pay attention, expecting God's presence here, now.

Expectant. "Our biggest enemy is contentment," said a frustrated pastor. "My folks think our church is already fulfilling all of the purposes of the church, just as we are. We're too easily pleased, too content with what we're doing now, not expecting more."

Alert. "I've been going to church all my life, so I've heard most of the scripture at one time or another. I've therefore found it helpful, just before the pastor reads the text on Sunday morning, to say a little prayer, 'Lord, surprise me. Show me something that I never saw before. Go ahead, shock me. I can take it.'"

Pay Attention. "Watching the evening news on TV is so depressing! Just one terrible event after another. Because I'm a Christian, I try to watch the news and keep asking, 'Is God behind any of this?' Is there some story that's so amazing, so unexpected, amid all the bad news, that there's no way to explain it except that God is involved in it, using people for good in a world of so much bad?"

Stay Awake. "We just passed each other in the hall at work and I mumbled 'Morning. How're you doin'?' and I heard him say, 'Alright, I guess. Stuff going on at home.' And we both moved on down the hall to our offices. But something, maybe it was God, I don't know, something made his words stick in my brain. I wondered if he was trying to say more to me than he said. So just before lunch I dropped in his office and tried to be direct and asked, 'Are you okay? Want to talk about the stuff at home?' Well, he opened up to me, got emotional. We talked for an hour. He's just a kid and feels he's in over his head. I had a short prayer with him and went on my way. Next morning I see him and he says, 'Thanks. You may have saved my life.' Thank God I noticed."

Signs of God's Presence Here and Now. "I came to church that Sunday discouraged, angry. It was the weekend when George Floyd was killed. Again? Really? Will this country ever learn? The service began. And after the opening hymn our pastor stood before us, planted her feet apart, and looked directly at us and said, with words strong and clear. 'I want you to hear me and mark what I say: God did not do this. This is not what God wants. We shall be judged. There's a new world coming and we're here this morning to get ready for it.' I haven't felt that close to God in a long time."

Hold on to your hats, Christ has come and is coming, maybe when you least expect. Your world all shook up, ready or not.

Chapter

2

Surprised

CHAPTER 2

Surprised

The beginning of the good news about Jesus Christ, God's Son, happened just as it was written about in the prophecy of Isaiah:

> Look, I am sending my messenger before you.
> He will prepare your way,
> a voice shouting in the wilderness:
> > "Prepare the way for the Lord;
> > make his paths straight."

John the Baptist was in the wilderness calling for people to be baptized to show that they were changing their hearts and lives and wanted God to forgive their sins. Everyone in Judea and all the people of Jerusalem went out to the Jordan River and were being baptized by John as they confessed their sins. John wore clothes made of camel's hair, with a leather belt around his waist. He ate locusts and wild honey. He announced, "One stronger

> *than I am is coming after me. I'm not even worthy to*
> *bend over and loosen the strap of his sandals. I baptize*
> *you with water, but he will baptize you with the Holy*
> *Spirit."*
>
> (Mark 1:4-8)

Advent's apocalyptic shaking continues, not through the words of Jesus but rather through words about Jesus spoken by John the Baptizer, the one sent by God to prepare us for the advent of The Word.

All the Gospels agree, you can't get to Jesus without first hearing John the Baptist preach on the Second Sunday of Advent. John is a bridge from the Old Testament to the New. While John preaches about what's happening now and in the future, you can't make sense of him except by knowing what God has done before. Three Old Testament verses are enlisted and combined to explain who John the Baptizer is and what he's up to (Exodus 23:20; Malachi 3:1; and Isaiah 40:3). John dresses in wilderness clothing, like an Old Testament prophet (2 Kings 1:8; Zechariah 13:4). He doesn't dress in jeans and a T-shirt, just one of the guys. Nor does he wear a fancy, black pulpit robe that certifies vetting and approval by the bishop. John is the last wild, untamed, eccentric Old Testament prophet who prepares us for The Prophet, Jesus:

> Look, I am sending my messenger before you.
>   He will prepare your way,
> a voice shouting in the wilderness:
>   "Prepare the way for the Lord;
>   make his paths straight."

Advent is announced not in some beautifully proportioned church, but in the remote, untamed, uncivilized wilderness where it's hard to find your way, and some become lost. For Israel after the Exodus, the wilderness was a place of testing—tests that Israel often flunked. But wilderness was also a place where the Hebrews were forced to rely on God, compelled to live out of control of their destiny, to be sustained solely by God as they made their way through uncharted territory, taking a very long time to find their way home.

Advent is a wilderness adventure. The good news that John announces goes out to the wilderness rather than demands that the wilderness come to it. Some words are too true, too unmanageable to be fully contained in a temple, synagogue, or church. The Word of God can be heard at confined, established, sacred sites, to be sure. But the Word, the living Incarnate Word refuses to be exclusively relegated to a church. It reaches out, pushes out, even into the wilderness.

Some words are too true, too unmanageable to be fully contained in a temple, synagogue, or church.

Surprisingly, multitudes braved the perils of the wilderness to hear John's sermons. *Everyone in Judea and all the people of Jerusalem went out to the Jordan River and were being baptized by*

John. Josephus, the turncoat Jewish historian, reports that King Herod (who, Mark 6:20 says, enjoyed the preaching of John, though only God knows why) became alarmed that so many flocked to hear John's messianic message. Lackey for the Roman overlords, Herod worried that a revolution might be whipped up by such wild talk. Anybody could tell that when John spoke of a mighty one who came after him, he was waxing messianic. (The Messiah for many in the first century was a military and political leader who would finally come in, raise an army, and rout the Romans, giving them what they deserved.) No wonder Herod got nervous that John's sermons drew big crowds.

BEGINNING

The beginning of the good news about Jesus Christ, God's Son. Creation begins with the first book of the Bible. Genesis = "beginning." If God didn't like to start things, there would be nothing. For there to be something, rather than nothing, there must be a God who creates, initiates, begins. It's Advent; brace yourself for the shock of the new.

While John the Baptist dresses like the prophets of old and is explained by quotes from Old Testament prophets (suggesting that his news is not completely new), John's message is not merely a reframing, reiteration, or repetition of what was said before. John's appearance and message in the wilderness presage a truly fresh start.

Don't miss the "news" in good news. The gospel is not, in the Greek, *photismos* (enlightenment), or *musterion* (an indescribable mystery), *gnosis* (secret knowledge that a wise one whispers into your ear), or *nomos* (rules and regulations that, by following, will make our life turn out right). The gospel is *euangelion*. Good news.

In opening his Gospel with "the beginning," Mark says that the advent of Christ is Genesis 1 all over again. Gradual human improvement, steady forward movement, taking one cautious step at a time, will not get us where we need to be. Our salvation requires some fresh intervention from the outside. A shake-up. We need a God who doesn't mind showing up, stepping in, and doing for us what we can't do for ourselves. New birth. Day one. Genesis 1 redone.

The advent of Christ is Genesis 1 all over again.

And yet, the God who makes a fresh beginning in the advent of Christ is the same God who was God all along. The Incarnation (God in human flesh) is not God's novel act of desperation when everything else God tried before didn't work. Stumped by our terrible sin, God said, "I've got an idea! I'll take on human flesh and be born of a virgin! Maybe that will finally grab their attention."

No. Christ wasn't a new and improved God come to us after the former God didn't live up to our expectations. Jesus's advent is not God's Plan B after God's Plan A failed. Christ was God all along, what God was up to from the very first. In the Old Testament, all the way back to the prophet Jeremiah, God had said, "You will be my people, and I will be your God" (Jeremiah 30:22). Some of the prophets had insisted that there would be a day when God, who had from the first wanted us to turn, return to God, would decisively step in, stunningly self-reveal, and turn to us. *Just as it was written about in the prophecy of Isaiah....*

In Mary's baby named Jesus, Joshua, meaning "God saves," God is doing what God had always done for Israel—saving God's people. God did not become something in Jesus that God was not already. From the first days of human history, God loves to take the bad news about us and make it into God's good news. Jesus comes to us not because our sin is so bad that God finally has to do something dramatic. Jesus comes to us because that's what the Father, Son, and Holy Spirit have always done— reaching out to us, lifting up the lowly, and casting down the proud and mighty. God takes on flesh, our flesh, because God has always been God with us, for us.

There's never been a better poem to describe what God's up to than Psalm 139. I'm sure that John the Baptist, and most of those to whom John preached, knew this psalm by heart. From the cradle to the grave, we can't be rid of God's seeking, searching love:

> LORD, ...
> *You know when I sit down and when I stand up.*
> *Even from far away, you comprehend my plans....*
> *You surround me—front and back....*

Where could I go to get away from your spirit?
    Where could I go to escape your presence?
If I went up to heaven, you would be there.
    If I went down to the grave, you would be there too!
If I could fly on the wings of dawn,
    stopping to rest only on the far side of the ocean—
        even there your hand would guide me;
        even there your strong hand would hold me
        tight!
If I said, "The darkness will definitely hide me;
    the light will become night around me,"
    even then the darkness isn't too dark for you!…
    you knit me together while I was still in my mother's
    womb.…
Your eyes saw my embryo,…
God, your plans are incomprehensible to me!
    Their total number is countless!…
    If I came to the very end—I'd still be with you.
            (Psalm 139:1-2, 5, 7-12, 16-18)

"I will be your God and you will be mine" from the embryo to the grave, earthly beginning to eternal end, is the same God to whom John points. Every advent of God, between the first Advent and next, is a reiteration of the psalmist's question, "Where could I go to get away from your spirit? Where could I go to escape your presence?"

Mark's Gospel has none of Matthew's or Luke's narration of the virgin birth of Jesus, no wise men or shepherds or babe in the manger or mysterious star in the sky. In a sense, John the Baptist's sermon is Mark's equivalent to Luke's Nativity. Here is the beginning, the birth of a way of God being God with us, something so fresh and new that we must prepare for the jolt. God is making good on God's ancient promises to Israel, but this time showing up in a way we didn't expect. Hold on to your hats; the Lord is coming, ready or not, in places unimaginable, accomplishing the inconceivable (no pun intended).

It's Advent. Be prepared to be surprised by God.

PREPARE

One of the most demanding aspects of travel is preparation. What to take on the trip? What to leave behind? Above all, how to be prepared for unexpected eventualities?

When Billy Graham selected our little Greenville, South Carolina, as the site for one of his citywide crusades, I don't remember much about the services themselves. Of course, I was only a kid at the time. What I remember most is the *two years* of preparation for the Billy Graham crusade. Our congregation breathlessly prepared as if Billy were going to drop in tomorrow. Churches were required to vote on whether or not to participate, to pony up funds to support the costs, hold hundreds of *weekly* prayer meetings all over town. By the time Billy finally arrived to save our fair city, he couldn't fail. We were already so worked up—prepared to direct traffic, usher, collect funds, hand out leaflets, lead others down to the front upon hearing the first notes of "Just As I Am," take down names of converts, set up post-crusade gatherings—that all Billy needed to say to have a successful sermon was "Hello. I'm Billy Graham."

When someone responds to the church's Advent announcement with "God has never shown up for me," it's not unreasonable to say, "Maybe God has, but you weren't prepared to be surprised. Because you thought you'd seen everything of God, you missed Advent."

In one of my early congregations, a Sunday school class studied the appointed lectionary readings for each Sunday the week before they were to be read and preached. After delivering my Sunday sermon, I'd hand out a simple questionnaire to the class who had prepared themselves by looking at the scripture beforehand and to a random sample of those who had not. Of course, those who had made some preparation retained twice as much of the substance of the sermon (and appreciated the sermon thrice as much) as those who were unprepared to be walloped by the Word.

In another congregation, there was a member who rarely attended services. She went through a tough time in her life. Loss of a job, sickness, and marital distress, one blow after another, laid her low. She required extensive treatment for her emotional break. My heart went out to her. When I commented to one of our more steadfast church members that I was concerned about Martha, the woman replied, "Poor thing. Martha has come to a time in her life when she was dying of thirst. She was forced to let down her bucket. Bless her heart, her well is dry. She failed to do her homework before the big exam."

Mark encapsulates John's sermon in a few words:

> *"Prepare the way for the Lord;*
> *make his paths straight."*

Prepare! Get ready!

John, let me ask you, as a fellow preacher, is "Prepare!" enough material for an entire Advent sermon?

I guess much depends on that for which you're preparing. Nobody needs to be told "Prepare to be bored to death by another dull sermon" or "Get ready to be confirmed in what you've always thought." No preparation is needed, no straight path is required, if you intend to walk in the direction you've always walked.

The philosophy professor began the class, "Existential philosophy is tough to understand. I'm not smart enough or entertaining enough to hand it over to you on my own. If you take this class, you must accept some responsibility for the class. Can't find time to do the reading? No point in showing up for my pitiful lectures."

John the Baptizer appears out in the middle of nowhere and says to the gathered throngs, "I've got just one thing to say to you, *Prepare!*" Implied in John's short, hortatory sermon is the admonition, "Here comes Jesus! Get ready to change direction, be surprised, all shook up, turned upside down! Prepare!"

When we prayed, "Where could I go to get away from your spirit? Where could I go to escape your presence?" we were surprised that included even the wilderness, even the words of a strangely attired preacher named John.

SURPRISE

John is the advance man, the announcer, the one who warms up the audience before the star attraction. Judged from the content of his introductory remarks, the next act, the One who comes after John who is so much mightier than he, must be quite a surprise.

How different is the sermon of John from many of the sermons of mainline, old-line, rapidly being sidelined North American Christianity. Who needs to prepare to hear a preacher say, in effect, "Let me introduce you to Jesus whom you already think you know. As you know, Jesus is a very nice, moderate person who is a lot like you. He will tell you what you have always wanted to hear, confirm what you have always believed, and walk alongside you in whatever direction you are most comfortable walking."

No need to take a bath, comb your hair, and come to church at an inconvenient hour of the week (or trot out into the threatening wilderness, be baptized, and risk upsetting King Herod) to hear that sermon. You could write that sermon yourself. In fact, in a weird way, you have.

I entered a church service a few weeks ago where we were led in an opening liturgy, "We have come here as the anxious, the hurting, the troubled, and those who are full of stress." Look at us.

The worship leader then urged us to breathe deeply, to center ourselves, and get comfortable. In other words, the purpose of this gathering is to tell you what you already know and to keep you on the road you're already walking. We are convened to affirm the "god" whom you were worshipping before you got dressed and came to church. "God" is what you call whatever therapy you find to be most reassuring.

No preparation is needed for the advent of a god that we've made up on our own.

The pilot's voice comes over the PA and reassuringly murmurs, "Welcome aboard, folks. Settle in and make yourselves comfortable for our uneventful flight to New York." John's sermon is more akin to that disturbing interruption when, midflight, the pilot awakens us and blurts out, "Everybody check your seat belts. We could be in for some rough weather."

The best Christmas sermon I ever heard was from the pastor who stood up on Christmas Eve and simply said to his congregation. "Tonight I have some breaking news."

Then he leaned into the microphone for good effect and said, "Good news. Tonight, the invasion has begun. We're about to be liberated." He sat down and we sang Christmas carols like our lives depended on it, which of course, they do.

Sorry if you thought God was a projection of your fondest wishes and deepest desires, a technique for getting whatever it is that you think you need more than God. One comes to us whom we did not expect. Your world is about to be rocked. Don't be surprised that you are surprised.

REPENT

John "preaches baptism." What's that? Baptism means everything that water means: birth (we spend nine months in water before we're born and our birth begins with the "breaking of the waters"); death (only a teaspoon can bring instant, suffocating death by drowning); refreshment, fun (who doesn't enjoy a party where they toss you into the swimming pool?); liberation (Israel could only initiate the Exodus if God parted the sea); life (whether you're a creationist or an evolutionist, you believe that life began in water). Baptism means all that in the name of Christ. God's word in water.

When you join Rotary, they hand you a lapel pin, give you a handshake, and offer you lunch. There is a Rotary Creed, fairly mild stuff, affirming integrity, service, blah, blah. I doubt anybody has ever refused to wear the pin out of their doctrinal disagreement with the Rotary Pledge.

But when you are initiated into the body of Christ, like John, we strip you down, bathe you, half drown you, pull you up all wet and sticky like a newborn, lay hands on your head, give you a job way beyond your natural abilities, insist that you affirm the Apostles' Creed—even when you don't understand all of it—and call you by the name *Christian*. You are asked to believe, or at least be open to believing, that God Almighty was born; that a virgin birthed Jesus; that Jesus's arrival was announced by a wild-eyed, crazily attired wilderness preacher; that he who was king allowed himself to be tortured to death; that his once-dead body came back to life after three days; and that the first thing on Jesus's mind on the day of Resurrection was to resume conversation with the same losers who betrayed and abandoned him in his time of trouble, promising to give them everything he had and heaven too.

Don't say you weren't warned.

Baptism is something done to you rather than by you, just like your salvation. The work baptism wants to perform in you is way beyond self-help. You can't do your own baptism, any more than you can save yourself from drowning by pulling yourself out of the water by your own hair. As a sacrament, baptism is a gift of God (grace = gift) whereby God—knowing that we are animals—uses the ordinary, bodily stuff of mundane creaturely life to get through to us. God turned toward us in creaturely ways that we animals comprehend, offering us love we've never fully understood.

Nobody is born Christian. You come into this faith only through gifts, by being adopted. Water + the story of Jesus told by Mark's Gospel + God rewriting your story + your willingness to be written into the story of Jesus = Christian. In baptism, you are not the sole author of the narrative of your life. God has not left up to you the burden of crafting your significance. (How much did you contribute to your first birth?) You don't have to struggle to figure out who you are; in baptism, the church names you, tells you what your life means, laying on you a name that's too much for you to bear on your own, *Christian.*

In baptism, you are not the sole author of the narrative of your life. God has not left up to you the burden of crafting your significance.

Without much debate, the church baptized the children of Christian parents, promising God we would bring up children as if they were Christians until they acted like it. To be sure, it's absurd to call a little baby, squalling and indignant, "Christian." Yet that's just what the church does until, sooner or later, the promises of baptism are fulfilled; we have become that person whom the church promised we would be. Somebody calls out "Christian," and we answer because, by the grace of God, the name fits.

It's a comfort, particularly during rough times, to know that, in baptism, God has taken responsibility for your salvation. Even though we don't always think like Christians, much less act like it, by baptism God promises to go ahead and be our God anyway. Even though you are sometimes unloving, unlovable, and often unbearable, the church, by baptism, promises to put up with you to the end and, at your end, relights the Baptism Candle, posting it by your coffin, as we give you back to the God who gave you to us.

John preaches baptism before he speaks of repentance because repentance (Greek, *metanoia*, close cousin of "metamorphosis," turning around and turning toward God) is not something that you do but rather something God does in you. You turn to God, not because you've come to your senses and have finally decided to get your life together, fly right, think right, because you feel it's right. You turn to God only because God in Christ has first turned to you.

When you hear Mark's report that John called *for people to be baptized to show that they were changing their hearts and lives and wanted God to forgive their sins*, it's understandable for you to think

John the Baptizer is handing you a new homework assignment. But you'd be wrong.

John's short sermon is not more bad news of all the things you simply must do if you are to set things right between you and God. What you're hearing is *The beginning of the good news about Jesus Christ, God's Son.*

We're not expected to repent, turn around, metamorphose ourselves so that God will notice us. We are to let God come to us, to allow ourselves to be loved. We repent, turn over a new leaf, not because we are trying to get right with God but because we believe John the Baptizer's sermon is true: Surprise! God in Christ is setting things right between us and God.

To be sure, *changing their hearts and lives* denotes transformation. But please note: change in behavior is usually a post- rather than a pre-baptismal phenomenon. Baptism is a "sign" that sets the process of repentance in motion, establishing the conditions whereby we can change.

Be careful of boasting "I can decide to give my life to Christ" or "I can make a new beginning with God."

Repentance is an "I can't" experience. I can't climb up to God; God will have to condescend to me. I can't save myself, God must do it. I can't forgive myself for the wrongs I've committed against God and neighbor. God will have to show me how.

Some of the most dramatic life-turnarounds and liberations I've witnessed have been those that occurred under the ministrations of Alcoholics Anonymous (AA). Among the Twelve Steps of AA is repentance, the "I can't" move: "We admitted we were powerless over alcohol—that our lives had become unmanageable." An admission of powerlessness is quickly followed by "We came to believe that a Power greater than ourselves could restore us to sanity." Confessing "I can't" is the prelude to affirming "With God, yes I can."

Repentance is a gift, grace, not a heroic achievement. It's a fruit of baptism's sure sign that God loves us rather than a requirement that must be met by us before God will love us.

"We love because God first loved us" (1 John 4:19). God takes the first step. We are unable to begin anything on our own. Only God can initiate or sustain the conversation between us and God, often beginning a new dialogue with us by using some preacher like John to give us the good news: God isn't your enemy, carping critic, or demanding schoolmaster. God is love.

God isn't your enemy, carping critic, or demanding schoolmaster. God is love.

To embrace John's news, to kick off your sandals and wade into the water, to honestly admit to the wilderness otherwise known as your hometown, to be open to God's turning your world and your life upside down, is to be open to loss. Something is gained, yes, in getting in step with God, in taking up residence in this new realm whose advent John announces. But much can be lost as well. And the loss could be painful. Repentance is an "I can't" experience in which we let go of our tight grip upon the present and forsake our usual way of getting what we want out of the world.

There's no way to begin worshipping Jesus without ceasing our bowing and scraping to some false god. Early Christians weren't persecuted for saying "Jesus Christ is Lord." They were martyred for saying that Caesar isn't.

Baptism is not only washing but also washing away. Advent repentance changes the question from "What are you giving this Christmas?" to "What are you giving up?" What might God take from you in making advent with you?

"Once I forsook my fantasy of having a painless, stress-free life, learning to follow Jesus was easy," she said.

"I thought what I needed most was better balance in my life," said the college student. "Then God showed me that what I call 'balance' was just my illusion that my life could be lived completely under my control."

I can't. God, you'll have to do it for me.

CHANGE

John the Baptizer's intent for his wilderness congregation is not just agreement but conversion. *Change.* My church used to go out and convert people, try to change their minds, argue, cajole, and persuade them into the truth of Christ.

Nowadays, we seem to have lost faith in the ability of the Holy Spirit to change hearts and minds. My church has self-divided into "traditionalists" and "progressives," each group trying to get as far apart from the other as possible because they believe very different things about same-sex unions. Irreconcilable differences, they say. The only thing they agree on is that the Holy Spirit is unable to change people once their mind is made up. Poor Jesus. He is now incapable of producing church with a mix of Republicans and Democrats, unable to entice them into taking Eucharist together whether they like one another or not. Best Jesus can do is to huddle together folks who look and think like one another.

"I'm so tired of arguing about human sexuality, they'll never change their left-wing views. Let 'em go. Leave our church so we can have church with those whose values are like mine."

Or "This church is full of homophobic, racist conservatives. I'm leaving."

If our fellow Christians are wrongheaded and confused, what's the response to that? Not sifting out the saints until there's nobody there but people who think as they thought before they came to church. The answer is in John the Baptizer's call to *metanoia*: conversion, change, renovation, repentance.

There's a new world coming. Let go of your tight grip on the old cosmos, relinquish your citizenship in the old order, and risk taking up residence in the new. Repent!

After service, a layperson grouses, "You preachers never talk about anything that's related to my world."

I try to find a nice way to say, "Scripture (and any of my sermons, if they're biblical) doesn't want to relate to your world. Scripture wants to rock your world."

While watching a Duke quarterback wolf down a near-lethal amount of steak at the lunch I paid for, I asked, "What do you think of what we do on Sundays at Duke Chapel?"

"I don't think about it," he responded with his mouth full. "Never been in the chapel."

"You've been a student here for three years and have never attended a service at the chapel?" I said, pushing my chair back from the table in indignation. "God give me patience!"

"Right. Never felt the need. I went to church some when I was a kid. From what I can remember, Christians are always trying to get people to change, to be different. I'm happy with my life the way it is right now, so I don't see the need. Are you going to eat those fries?"

"That's a surprisingly intelligent reason not to come to church," I marveled. "I shall do that in needlepoint, frame it, and put it over the chapel's front door, just under the statue of John Wesley—*Achtung!* God at work. Dare not enter this chapel if you're averse to emerging as a different person because you're living in a whole new world."

Jesus may take us "Just as I am," as we sang with Billy Graham. But Jesus never, ever leaves us as we are. A young plumber once timidly told me that Jesus had surprised him one night as he was coming home late from work. "As real as you please. There he was. Standing in front of me, on my back porch, like he had been waiting, like he needed me for something."

When I asked why he had never told anyone about the back porch advent, he replied, "If what I saw was really real, if Jesus is true, if he wanted me, then I couldn't keep being the same as I am. I love my wife and family. My life is okay as it is, so I couldn't afford to admit that Jesus is real or I'd have to be a different me."

John the Baptizer announces not just a change of heart, but the advent of a whole new world, the recognition of which is bound to result in a new you.

"This is Michael," our teacher announced to our sixth-grade class. A frightened-looking, blond little boy stood before us. "He is from Poland. Class, you can help him learn English. He is a displaced person."

What's that?

"Michael has had to leave his homeland and come here to America, because of the war and all. He's been displaced. Michael, take your seat."

"Poland must really suck for a kid to have to come to Greenville in order to have a good life," a classmate whispered to me across the aisle.

We tried to do what we could to relate to the displaced person. He rapidly got the hang of English and schoolyard softball. But there was one problem: he stole food. A Twinkie would disappear from someone's lunchbox. Somebody's sandwich went missing. One day, the displaced person was caught in the act. Responding to our complaints, the teacher opened Michael's desk. Old, stale sandwiches, apples, and Fig Newtons were packed in the desk.

"Michael, you must not take other people's food. Do you understand me?" Teacher said.

Michael nodded but, just as we predicted, next day, there was Janie in tears because her slice of chocolate pie that her grandmother had given her was gone.

"Michael!" said our teacher as she shook the displaced person. "Stop stealing food. You are not in Poland anymore.

You are in America. America. There's enough food here for everybody. I promise you that you'll not be hungry ever again. You need food, all you've got to do is ask. Do you hear me? You're not in Poland anymore."

And I tell you, Michael's eyes grew wide, he silently nodded as if he finally understood. He never again took anybody's food. He was different, displaced no more, his eyes had been opened and he had become a naturalized citizen of a new country. Michael had awakened to a whole new world.

Something very much like that is what John the Baptizer wants to work in you.

"How on earth did you survive?" I asked her. She and her family had suffered terribly under the Communist dictatorship of Romania. They were denied access to medical care, kicked out of their government housing, and she was forced to leave school, all because they dared to criticize the government.

"My mother and father told us, 'We can't oust the Communists, but we can start living as if the government has already fallen. Be sure,' they told us, 'one day this nightmarish regime will end. But right now, our family will go ahead and start living as if that day is already here.' That's how we not only survived, we triumphed."

It's Advent. God is on the way. Maybe today, or tomorrow, or a thousand years from now, God will have God's way with the world, what was begun in Genesis shall be brought to completion. John the Baptizer invites us to metamorphose, to repent, to begin living in the light of that final, decisive advent.

If what John the Baptist preaches is true, then you've got to change, repent, allow yourself to be turned upside down, or risk looking ridiculously out of step with the regime change that John announces. Come on, make King Herod nervous. Be baptized, begin being the revolution.

Baptism explains why, when Jesus's ministry got going soon after John's sermon, and Jesus began calling disciples, disruptive Jesus was a notorious home-wrecker. Nobody follows Jesus without, to some degree, disobeying the Fifth Commandment. In my years as Dean of the Chapel I had maybe twenty anxious phone calls from parents: "Help! I sent my child to Duke to be a success and she has become a religious fanatic!"

"Religious fanatic" in this case defined as someone who, rather than graduating law school, instead ran away with the Catholics to a literacy program in Haiti.

"Hey, lady, I'm from Greenville, home of Bob Jones University. Catholics in Haiti ain't fanaticism." These parents may be ignorant of the specifics of the Christian faith, may have never heard of John the Baptist, but at least they know enough to tremble when one of their upwardly mobile, bred-for-success kids comes home after Christmas vacation and says, "I heard this preacher named John. What he said really shook me. I've decided that I don't want to live where you raised me to live. I want a different future."

That young woman wants to be a citizen of a whole new world.

Repentance is not so much feeling sorry for all the ways you've screwed up (though it's big of you to feel bad about that).

Repentance is simply waking up and acknowledging the facts of life now that God has turned toward us, accepting reality and living in accord with it. The Advent, gospel truth: God has turned toward us. The Advent response: When God turns toward you, and you turn toward God, your life turns around.

From what I've observed, if you are reasonably content with the world as it is, if your life is manageable and you're not too troubled by the state of the world, and you don't feel too much of your neighbor's pain, remaining happy as a pig in mud, then you are unlikely to join those multitudes who braved the wilderness to hear a wild prophet preach for *people to be baptized to show that they were changing their hearts and lives and wanted God to forgive their sins.*

On the other hand, if God has blessed you with some holy discontent, if you expect that this world, as good as it often is, is not as good as it *could* get, if you find it difficult to sleep at night after you've seen the gaunt faces of those hungry children on the news, or you get so angry you could scream when you see the bruises under the makeup of the woman next to you in the grocery store checkout line, then John's two-point sermon—"God's about to shake things up" and "Get ready, get washed up to show that you've been shook up"—is good news.

By the way, repentance is not a one-and-done experience. In baptism, the old sinful Adam is put to death (Romans 3:19-22). Yet, as Martin Luther noted, the Old Adam is a mighty good swimmer. Each day you wake up, jump out of bed, and submit to the continuing work of repentance begun in your baptism. Though the rite of baptism takes only a few minutes to perform, it takes your whole life to finish what was begun in you when the church doused you "in the name of the Father, the Son, and the Holy Spirit" and called you Christian. We never get too mature, or so adept at following Jesus that there's no need daily to keep turning to the God who, in Christ, has turned to you.

UNEXPECTED GOD

Who is God? Where is God? What's God up to? And what does God want from us? On any given Sunday, these God questions roam among the souls of the congregation.

Maybe that's why John's wilderness message is not primarily about our repentance. It's mostly about God's advent.

> One stronger than I am is coming after me. I'm not even worthy to bend over and loosen the strap of his sandals. I baptize you with water, but he will baptize you with the Holy Spirit.
>
> (Mark 1:7-8)

John bends over backward to make explicit that he is not the main event, not the source of good news. While John baptizes with water, the One who comes *will baptize you with the Holy Spirit*. Matthew 3:11 and Luke 3:16 highlight that the Spirit's descent is judgment upon us. These scriptures say that the Messiah's baptism will be "with the Holy Spirit and with fire." Their John is preacher of coming fire-and-brimstone judgment (Matthew 3:11; Luke 3:17). But not Mark.

Mark has no Pentecost descent of the Holy Spirit on the church (Acts 2) or Jesus breathing Spirit upon the disciples on

Easter evening (John 20). In the Baptizer's sermon in Mark, the Spirit is a gracious God actively turned toward us, God with us.

Mark's Baptizer preaches grace rather than judgment, the descent of the Holy Spirit as the near presence of God rather than primarily the Spirit as purifying, judging fire. Sure, repentance, change is preached, but it's in response to the good news that the kingdom has now come near (Mark 1:15). ("Where could I go to get away from your spirit?" comes to mind.) As the Fourth Gospel puts it, "The Word became flesh and made his home among us" (John 1:14). The interesting thing about John's sermon is not its location (wilderness) or that it stresses what we are to do (repent), but that it asserts God's relocation, God's Advent action: here comes God.

John preaches that this One who comes is *One stronger than I.* But if Jesus is powerful, more powerful than John the forerunner prophet, it is not self-evident. Later in their ministries, when John was in prison and Jesus was busy inaugurating his reign, Matthew's John the Baptist sent some of his disciples to ask, "Are you the one who is to come, or should we look for another?" (Matthew 11:3). Even John, the one who announced the surprise of Christ's advent, is surprised that the One who came was powerful in a different way from the Messiah he expected.

Ask folks what they think of God before they meet Jesus and they're likely to speak of God's remoteness. God is way up there, and we are stuck down here. Incarnation, the enfleshment of God as Jesus of Nazareth, on the other hand, says that in Jesus Christ, God gets up close and personal. "Gospel," good news is not only words about Jesus, it's Jesus. Bodily present. Jesus didn't just preach the gospel; he was the gospel. More than a new set of ideas, helpful principles, or a wise philosophy, John announces the advent of a person.

I wonder if we depersonalize God into dry doctrines, abstract principles, or vague ideas in a vain attempt to get a personal God off our backs. You can embrace an idea, but no idea will ever embrace you. You can be enthusiastic over an abstract notion, but no impersonal abstraction can evoke your obedience, much less your love.

Dietrich Bonhoeffer said that the purpose of preaching is to allow the person of Christ to walk among Christ's people. I like that. Preaching as not merely an auditory, but also a bodily phenomenon as Christ roams free in the church.

Paul's favorite term for the church is the body of Christ, Christ taking up room in the world, Christ discontent to remain secluded in heaven. Jesus comes to us, taking up room in the world, walking with us.

Years ago, the scholars of the errant "Jesus Seminar" made a heroic effort to identify the words of scripture that were likely the actual words of Jesus. They didn't find many. Some of us responded, "Who told you that Christians worship the words of Jesus? We're in love with Jesus."

By implication, if we want to be close to Jesus, it's good to place ourselves physically, bodily near him. Prepare for the advent of Christ by locating yourself as close as you can to where Christ is likely to show up.

"Why am I here each morning spreading sandwiches for the homeless?" he answered in response to my question. "I'll tell you. I'm not that great a Christian or a good believer. I learned early on that if I was going to make it as a Christian, I'd have to go where Christ is. Like Sunday morning church. Like here in this ministry to the homeless." Prepare the way of the Lord.

We preachers join John the Baptist in preparing a road, a straight path for our listeners to get to God and for God to get to them, enabling the risen Christ to walk among Christ's people.

HERE COMES GOD

John's sermon, though short, may be hard for us to hear since many of us have come to believe that church, worship, the concerns of scripture are mostly about us. We arrive at church with our set of questions we want answered, personal dilemmas that must be solved, and assorted errands (emotional, political, and financial) for God to run in our behalf.

"That service didn't do a thing for me," we mutter as we head to the parking lot after church. "Didn't get nothin' out of the sermon."

Church is where we come, not to be encountered by the God who advents to us, but rather where we take an even deeper dive into our own subjectivity. I think about God, therefore there must be one. I am the judge of all truth. Reality is whatever works for me. To John's assertion, "God is coming, God is here," we respond, "But that's not the way I see it." End of the discussion.

Rather than humans being creations of God, God becomes the imaginative creation of human beings, a projection of our fondest desires and deepest needs. *Humanity uttered in a loud voice* was the way theologian Karl Barth put it, a God who looks suspiciously like us.

If you ever wondered why the twentieth century was one of the bloodiest, or why the twenty-first is off to such a lousy start, here's your answer. Once we refashioned God in our own imaginations, there was no one left to stand against human willfulness and sin. The god that we had made in our own image had nothing to say that disturbed or jolted us, or called our actions into question.

"I refuse to be a part of a church that espouses values different from mine." And so, he left his church, refusing the adventure of God's making him a different person than he was before he came to church.

Our self-made god is full of acceptance and love, never judgment or condemnation, certainly never punishment. This god, being constructed out of our own omnivorous need would never expect repentance, much less insist that you be born again (John 3:16). "Dear, I love you just the way you are. Promise me you won't change a thing."

We don't expect God to address us through the voice of a shabbily dressed, wilderness preacher crying, "Wash up! Change! Get ready for God!" These days we backpack into the wilderness not expecting (or even wanting) God to show up but rather in order to spend more time alone with ourselves.

All I'm saying is that there are lots of reasons why you may not resonate with the preaching of John the Baptizer, reasons having nothing to do with John's Jewishness, strange clothing, or with words that are two thousand years old.

Close to 95 percent of Americans are willing to believe God is. Very few believe that God is a Jew from Nazareth who not only took upon Godself our human flesh and daily cares but also came to us even out in our wilderness where he was baptized and then tempted along with the rest of us, suffered rejection, torture, and death worse than any of us, and who, even after we so disappointed God, returned to us, so eager was God to have us.

Every religion offers to help us finite creatures climb up to or dig deeper into the infinite and the eternal. Only Christianity contends that the infinite and eternal God descended, took time for us, and became one of us, taking the form of our finitude—Incarnation.

Every religion offers to help us finite creatures climb up to or dig deeper into the infinite and the eternal. Only Christianity contends that the infinite and eternal God descended, took time for us, and became one of us, taking the form of our finitude—Incarnation. John the Baptizer preached the surprisingly good news that we need not climb up to God; in Jesus Christ, God comes down to us, taking time for us, staying with us, even though we didn't know how to stay with God.

Incarnation is the church at its most counterintuitive in its claims about God's love at its most outrageous. Listen to John's Advent sermon that's hard for nine out of ten Americans to believe: even though we could not avail ourselves of God, the true and living God lovingly became available to us. By God's grace, there's still time. Repent!

There's no doubt that God will be with us (read the Bible!). How much more does God need to say or do to convince us, "I *will* be your God"? (Jeremiah 30:22, emphasis added). The only question is that implied by John the Baptist's sermon: will we be with God?

Chapter

3

Light

Light

A man named John was sent from God. He came as a witness to testify concerning the light, so that through him everyone would believe in the light. He himself wasn't the light, but his mission was to testify concerning the light....

This is John's testimony when the Jewish leaders in Jerusalem sent priests and Levites to ask him, "Who are you?"

John confessed (he didn't deny but confessed), "I'm not the Christ."

They asked him, "Then who are you? Are you Elijah?"

John said, "I'm not."

"Are you the prophet?"

John answered, "No."

> *They asked, "Who are you? We need to give an answer*
> *to those who sent us. What do you say about yourself?"*

> *John replied,*

> "I am a voice crying out in the wilderness,
>   Make the Lord's path straight,
>   just as the prophet Isaiah said."

> *Those sent by the Pharisees asked, "Why do you baptize*
> *if you aren't the Christ, nor Elijah, nor the prophet?"*

> *John answered, "I baptize with water. Someone greater*
> *stands among you, whom you don't recognize. He comes*
> *after me, but I'm not worthy to untie his sandal straps."*
> *This encounter took place across the Jordan in Bethany*
> *where John was baptizing.*
>
> (John 1:6-8, 19-28)

When God shakes heaven and earth and shows up among us, most of us fail to recognize Jesus Christ as God with us. Jesus looks too much like one of us. Then we hear Jesus's teaching, see Jesus's work, and our verdict is, "God wouldn't say things like that. That's not God, is it?"

> Sweet little Jesus boy,
> they made you be born in a manger.
> ("Sweet Little Jesus Boy" by Robert MacGimsey)

Jesus looked too much like us to chin up to our expectations for who God had to be if God were to be worthy of our worship. Thus John the Baptizer speaks of the One who comes after him as the One *whom you don't recognize.*

Matthew and Luke wrestle with the notion of Incarnation—Jesus Christ, fully God and completely human—by telling of Jesus's birth by the virgin, Mary. Mark doesn't mention the virginal conception of Jesus. John's Gospel takes a different tack from any of the others, waxing philosophical about "the Word became flesh." The Gospels talk in these ways about the advent of Jesus Christ in order to make a claim about the God/human Jesus, but also to be honest about us and the limits of our imaginations. From the beginning, many had difficulty seeing Jesus for who he really was. *Someone greater stands among you, whom you don't recognize.* Many prayed for God to come to us. Few if any expected God to show up as Jesus.

The bold Christian claim is that when we look at this Jew from Nazareth who lived briefly, died violently, and rose unexpectedly, we see as much of God as we ever hope to see.

The bold Christian claim is that when we look at this Jew from Nazareth who lived briefly, died violently, and rose unexpectedly, we see as much of God as we ever hope to see. Who is God? What is God up to in heaven and on earth? Look at this One who, even though we didn't recognize the Messiah at first, is the whole truth about God.

A group of students asked for a meeting with me, introducing themselves as the "Duke Spirituality Initiative." They said that they needed my help to establish a "Spirituality Center" in Duke Gardens.

"What's that?" I asked.

"It's a secluded section of the gardens, with appropriate plantings, and a bench. Whenever someone wants to be spiritual, they would go there and sit and meditate."

"Why would I be interested in creating such a place?" I asked. "I'm a Christian. When we want to get 'spiritual,' we don't sit by ourselves and stare at shrubbery. We get together with other people. Bodies. We believe in something called the Holy Spirit who loves to descend from heaven upon bodies. Ever heard the term 'Incarnation'?"

On the Third Sunday of Advent John's Gospel shuttles, in just five verses, from high-flown talk of "the Word" (John 1:1) down toward "a man named John" (1:6). We spiritual eager beavers, clambering up to the ethereal and heavenly, are quickly shifted back down to the solid stuff of God's good earth. God meets us on our turf. Heaven's movement, thanks to the Holy Spirit, is always downward, one-way traffic from God to humanity.

John's Gospel poetically praises the Word, the eternally begotten Son of God, the Word who was with God before the beginning of the world (John 1:1), as flesh, our human flesh. During the season of Advent, the Fourth Gospel says that a major way you gain access to an encounter with this Word is through the human voice of a preacher out in the wilderness, "a man named John."

The Fourth Gospel tells us little about this man John—nothing of his parentage or his hometown—only that he was "sent from God." Unlike John the Baptizer in the other Gospels, this Gospel's John the Baptist wears no odd clothing and issues no threatening call to "Repent!" He's not even called John the Baptist. In this Gospel John is just a "voice."

"Who are you?" nervous emissaries sent by the religious bigwigs demand. John replies, "I am a voice...."

SENT

The Fourth Gospel's John the Baptist is "a witness" who "testif[ies] concerning the light." Why? "So that through him everyone would believe in the light. He himself wasn't the light, but his mission was to testify concerning the light (John 1:6-8). Mark's John the Baptist calls upon people to be baptized and repent. On the Third Sunday of Advent, John's message, as remembered by the Gospel of John, sounds different.

John is no free agent who speaks for himself. He is "sent from God" as an emissary who testifies to "the light" (v. 7). This preacher doesn't "share himself" or give you a peek into what's "on his heart." John's authorization to witness is external. "Sent from God," John is commissioned by God to deliver a message about the dawning of light.

Today's preachers are successors to John the Baptist. We preach what we've been told to preach. The message may come through us, but it is not *from* us. We preach the word that we have received. Our message is externally derived and is validated and empowered by something more significant than our pleasing personalities or our way with words. "Sent from God." Maybe that's the most important thing to know about a preacher and not our theological education or credentials. A preacher is sent, speaks under external authorization and compulsion, and delivers a word that does not originate with the preacher.

I have found in my own preaching ministry that the most important survival tactic for a preacher is to keep remembering that you preach because you, like John the Baptist, have been sent. You didn't volunteer for this job. When questioned, or under threat by unhappy church folks, or when people impudently ask, "What gives you the right to say…?" your best defense is to respond simply but confidently, "I was sent. You think I would have willingly volunteered for this job? My being a preacher was God's idea before it was mine."

The congregation may pay my salary, but when my frail, aging, Southern-accented voice is speaking the sermon, I don't work for them nor am I finally accountable to them. Of course I'd like them to receive my sermon, but their hearing or not hearing doesn't validate my message.

All the Gospels portray John the Baptizer as the forerunner, the one who introduces Jesus and urges the multitudes to prepare for Christ's arrival. The Fourth Gospel's depiction of John is curious. John's telling seems to have nothing to do with John the Baptist's personal attributes, talents, or family background. While John is reputed to have been a fine preacher whose sermons were a big hit, the Gospel of John gives us next to nothing of the content of John's preaching.

In other Gospels, particularly Matthew and Luke, we are given a more detailed report of what John preached. There, John is a fierce prophet who pronounces dire warnings and gives his listeners specific things that they need to do in their daily lives that show that they are indeed turning around and repenting. But not in the Gospel of John. The focus here is on the messenger, The Voice. When John is asked to share what's most significant about himself, he replies, "I am a voice."

John's characterization of himself as "voice" reminds us that Christianity is an auditory phenomenon, an acoustical event involving the human voice. As Paul says, faith comes from hearing (Romans 10:17). Nobody hears the news about Jesus straight from heaven, at least nobody I've known. The news normally comes through the voices of earthly news broadcasters like John. "He came as a witness to testify concerning the light, so that through him everyone would believe in the light. He himself wasn't the light, but his mission was to testify concerning the light" (John 1:7–8). John is not so much an official spokesperson but rather is a "witness." In court, a witness testifies to what the witness has seen and heard. Nobody expects the witness to be creative or original. With a witness, the personality, educational background, or actions of the witness are unimportant to the court. What matters is the vocal testimony of the witness. The witness points away from herself toward an event that has occurred outside of the witness.

"Tell the jury what you heard at the corner of Fifth and Vine on the afternoon of Monday, December 11." The witness is expected truthfully to testify to an actual occurrence, not to engage in fantasy or wishful thinking. That's what John's Gospel and the Voice invite us to do as we stand on the threshold of the Incarnation. We are not only called to witness to the advent of the Babe of Bethlehem, but we are also called to be witnesses to what we've seen and heard, to stand and deliver, to testify to the reality of an event that has occurred, a gift that has been given.

The Messiah is not a concoction of our wishful thinking. The gospel is not something that we come up with by ourselves. Good news about Jesus is not derived from within us but is testimony to something that has happened to us.

Christians are not necessarily those who are more truthful than others, or more spiritually enlightened. Certainly we are not better people than others. We are simply those who have heard some surprising news, from the voice of someone sent from God, who tells us what God has done, is doing, will do among us. Then we tell everybody else all about it.

WITNESS

The one sent from God has only one function: to "witness." A witness is someone who testifies, gives an honest account of what the witness has seen and heard. Except for two brief references to this "witness" (John 5:33-36; 10:40-42), these few verses at the beginning are all that the Fourth Gospel tells about John. The Voice speaks and then he disappears. John has no continuing role or enduring significance other than the sound of his voice, a voice crying in the wilderness "that through him everyone would believe" (1:7).

"What did that strange young preacher tell you about God?" your buddy says to you as you return from the wilderness.

"Don't rightly remember. I do recall that when he preached, it was like a light switched on in my heart, and I got it."

"What exactly did he say about God?"

"Can't recollect anything specific. All I remember was that he said God was 'Light,' whatever that means. All I remember about the preacher is his name, John."

In one of my first churches, I wanted to learn more about what people retained from listening to my sermons. So, standing at the door bidding farewell to folks at the end of the service, I randomly handed out cards that said "List three things you remember from the sermon today."

The results were depressing. Few respondents could recollect more than one idea. Some of the ideas they claimed to remember were found nowhere in my sermon notes! Give me a break.

As I was sharing my disappointment with an African American preacher friend of mine, he replied, "Where did you white preachers get the notion that preaching is about ideas?"

Well, if not ideas, then what?

"Preaching is about getting people to a place where Jesus can get to them and they can get to Jesus," he responded. "Preaching hopes to provoke presence, bodily presence, Jesus showing up among us." Or, again Bonhoeffer: Preaching enables the risen Christ to walk among Christ's people.

John the Baptist, at least in the Fourth Gospel, didn't talk about fresh, new religious insights. He didn't call people to social action or suggest modifications in their behavior. He preached, "Look! The Lamb of God!" inviting people to see the Light, assuming that if he could just get listeners to look in the right direction, they would know how to respond to what they saw.

The theologian Karl Barth said that John is the model for every preacher of any time and place. John points away from himself toward Christ. If the listeners' vision doesn't go through the preacher and to Christ, if the preacher somehow becomes the main event and gets in the way of Christ, the preacher's sermon has misfired. John is a voice, a witness, someone who points toward the coming Christ. He is transparent, like a pane of clear glass, to the One who comes after him who is greater than he. Not a bad goal for any preacher.

The Fourth Gospel stunningly opens by calling Jesus the Word (in the Greek, *logos*) who was sent down from heaven and dwelled among us (John 1:9-14). As the Word, Christ is God's self-communication, the major means of the commencement of divine-human communion. Jesus was more than words can say, but never less than words. In Jesus, the words about God became God-in-the-flesh dwelling among us as the Word. Presence. Jesus is God's word to the world, God's sermon to us. As Paul put it, what we preachers preach is not ourselves, but Jesus Christ as Lord (2 Corinthians 4:5). John's Gospel employs a host of metaphors for Jesus—the door, the Good Shepherd, the vine, bread, water, life. But this richly metaphoric Gospel begins with

Jesus as the Word. "These things are written," says the Fourth Gospel, "so that you will believe" (John 20:31).

Jesus is God's word to the world, God's sermon to us.

The Word, which is not self-evident, is prone to incomprehension and misunderstanding. As John puts it, Jesus was such a shock, so surprising that "the light came to his own people, and his own people didn't welcome him" (John 1:11). Failure is everywhere possible for our words about the Word. Throughout John's Gospel, almost no one who is confronted by Christ, the Word Made Flesh, understands anything the Messiah is talking about. Jesus speaks to Nicodemus of the need to be born of the water and Spirit and Nicodemus, the supposedly wise teacher, thinks of natural birth. Jesus talks to the Samaritan woman at the well about living water come down from heaven, and she thinks water drawn up by a bucket. The crowds hear Jesus speak of "bread" and they think he's talking about what they had for breakfast.

"I preached at that church for six years, six years! And only one person ever came forward for baptism," lamented the preacher. Lamentably poor results for six years of sermons. Still, that preacher's record looks good compared with our Lord in John's Gospel.

Maybe the validity of the Word isn't to be measured merely by the number who nod ascent to it. Truth is still truth whether it makes sense to me or not. As a preacher, I marvel that, at least in the Fourth Gospel, Jesus seems unperturbed and undeterred by people's lack of comprehension of his words spoken. Jesus keeps talking, even if they rarely comprehend what he's talking about. Maybe understanding and comprehension are not the only goal of his teaching. Perhaps Jesus's chief desire is presence, simply to be God with us.

(O ye who can't make out a word of your preacher's sermons, take heart!)

Still, look at you. Here you are, reading words about the Word. Despite all the perfectly good reasons for not believing the testimony of a wild man with a voice like John's about a surprising savior like the Light, you believe. Mostly. Though you don't fully understand the doctrine of the Incarnation, you love Jesus enough to continue to follow Jesus even when you can't follow all that he says or comprehend completely who he is.

Love is rarely love if it's fully comprehensible. Loving and being loved by Jesus is a lot like that.

If you've ever been in love with someone (and if you haven't, I'm not enough of a poet to explain it to you), then you know that love is rarely love if it's fully comprehensible. Loving and being loved by Jesus is a lot like that.

A man said to me, "When I was a teenager, I heard a sermon, maybe it was at church camp, maybe it was at the church where

I was dating this girl, anyway, the preacher said something about, 'When God calls you, God calls you by your own name, not somebody else's name.' Never forgot that. Guess you could say it changed my life. Opened my eyes. I didn't understand what being a Christian was, but what I heard was better even than understanding. Though I can't remember the preacher's name."

"Was it John?" I asked.

The Incarnation, God's enfleshment, God Almighty showing up and surprising us in a sermon, is the great mystery that makes preaching possible. Preaching is a divinely wrought, miraculous act; God's speech. Preaching, for reasons known only to God, is God's chosen means of self-revelation. If a sermon "works," if you actually hear something in a sermon, in spite of your defenses or your preacher's homiletical limitations, it occurs as a gracious gift of God, a miracle somewhat akin to the virginal conception of Jesus by the Holy Spirit.

"What did you learn about preaching after listening to all those sermons?" I asked a friend. He had spent Sundays of his three-month sabbatical listening to other preachers.

"I learned that if anybody anywhere hears anything from a sermon, it's a miracle!"

One reason why Christians tend to believe in the likelihood of miracles like the virgin birth of Jesus or the resurrection of Christ is that we have experienced miracles of a similar order, if not the same magnitude, in our own lives as we have listened to a sermon. A word has surprised us from afar, something has been born in us that we ourselves did not conceive. It's a mysterious, undeserved divine gift. A miracle.

That's why it takes three to make a sermon work: a preacher, a listener, and the intervention of the Holy Spirit. Preaching is not only talk about God but miraculous talk by God. Hearing, really hearing a sermon requires external assistance. God, Father, Son, and Holy Spirit saying words to us through a preacher that we could never say to ourselves.

At the same time preaching is an utterly human, mundane, carnal, and fleshly undertaking. For Almighty God to speak to us, and to speak in ways that we comprehend, is an incarnational, God/human, Spirit/flesh exercise. A less secure, less sovereign and free godlet would never have risked verbal intercourse with us down on our level. To talk with us is to take up the sins of the world, to risk entanglement in our sinful evasion of the truth, and to put oneself in danger of being the victim of our violence if we hear something we don't want to hear. In the Incarnation, God took that risk. And next Sunday, in your preacher's sermon, God may risk incarnational conversation with you.

If Christ had not spoken to us, if he had limited his ministry to serene contemplative prayer or quiet walks in the woods, if he had stayed home and kept to himself, we would have had little reason to crucify him. We weren't opposed to Jesus until he opened his mouth. His words brought out the worst in us. Jesus told us the truth about God and we hated Jesus for it. "We're going to stop these words from this uppity preacher, even if we have to nail him to a cross to shut him up," we said in unison.

Didn't work. Three days later, Jesus strides forth from the tomb and resumes the conversation, whether we want him to or not.

"As I was saying before I was so rudely interrupted by the cross...."

Nothing can keep the Light from shining.

SEEING THE LIGHT, AGAIN

If you are reading this book, conscientiously preparing yourself for the Nativity, I expect that the declaration, "God is not as far away from us as we thought. God is coming to us, coming to stand beside us, Jesus Christ is born!" is no longer a surprise, no longer news. In a few days, we'll be standing on the eve of Christmas, an event that the shopping malls have been anticipating and announcing since Halloween. So part of our challenge in preparing to hear again the good news of Christmas is that, for many of us, it's no longer news.

Part of our challenge in preparing to hear again the good news of Christmas is that, for many of us, it's no longer news.

Can you remember when you were not a Christian? I can't, bless you if you can. I can't remember when I heard the Christmas story for the very first time. Maybe you can remember the first person who said to you, "Hey, Jesus Christ is born of Mary! God is not against us; God is with us!" I can't. I've known God with

Us, Emmanuel longer than I can remember. If Advent brings strange, unexpected, hard-to-understand news to you, I almost envy you.

Who bothers young children by discussing the atonement, or Christ's sacrifice, or the details of his agonizing death? But we eagerly recount to them the story of Christ's birth in Bethlehem, encouraging the kids to don bathrobes and take their parts in the annual Christmas pageant. They don't know the lines to "O For a Thousand Tongues to Sing," but they all know "O Little Town of Bethlehem." Most of us have known the good news of Christmas for a long, long time.

For those of you who, like me, can't remember when you didn't know about the Incarnation, for whom the good news no longer seems like news, one of the purposes of this book is to defamiliarize Advent, to show you something you may have missed, to speak about the wonder of Advent and Christmas wonder in such a way that the good news sounds like news once again.

All Christians are the receivers, not the originators, of this news. None of us came to the Light; the Light of the World came to us.

We ought to be reminded, therefore, that this good news is not innate. All Christians are the receivers, not the originators, of this news. None of us came to the Light; the Light of the World came to us.

Over my years as a pastor, I have stressed, in every congregation I have served, the importance of being a warm, welcoming congregation. Church is where we (to paraphrase Paul) "welcome others as you have been welcomed" (Romans 15:7).

Yet please note. John the Baptizer doesn't sit in Jerusalem, keep office hours, and welcome people to have a chat about God. John goes out to the wilderness to them. Just like Jesus. Church, in the light of John the Baptist, preacher of the Light, is not a "Come to us" sort of thing. "We'll come to you" is more in the spirit of John 1.

How do we know any of this? Only through witnesses like John who were sent from God to point us toward Light. God didn't wait for us to come to our senses, finally wake up, listen to our better angels, and move toward the Light. God sent Matthew, Mary, _____ (fill in the blank with the name of your particular witness) with the news. Somebody had to love Jesus enough, love us enough, to take the time to tell us the story, to live and walk in the light so that we were attracted to it.

"This is the friendliest church in town. When one of us is in need, we've got one another's back. We're a loving, caring, family here."

Sorry, that's not good enough for the God who, through the witness of John, came out and got us.

"We used to call ourselves 'evangelical,' but now that word is in disrepute, we prefer to be called 'traditionalists,' those who care for, defend, and protect scriptural authority and the orthodox traditions of the church," explained one church member as he busily conspired to split our church in two.

In love, I said, "I liked you better when you were known as 'evangelicals,' when you still cared about who hadn't gotten the news, before you just hunkered down on the news daring anybody to take it outside of the church! Jesus ordered you to let your light shine, not hide it under a basket."

The first Bible verse I learned by heart was John 3:16: "For God so loved the church and people who look a lot like me that...."

No! It's "God so loved *the world* that God gave God's only Son to...."

As the Voice says, the Light was the *light of all*. Through the light shining from the witness, some saw the Light (John 1:5)— not as many as Christ might like, but enough to make Herod nervous—and nothing the darkness has ever been able to throw at us has been able to silence the witnesses or put out the Light.

"I spent forty years of my life thinking God was mad at me," she said during a Bible study session. Thanks be to God that God sent her a witness. No way she could have heard the truth about God if someone had not loved Jesus and her enough to witness.

WITNESSES

John is only a "witness." *He himself* [John] *wasn't the light, but his mission was to testify concerning the light* (John 1:8). That's what John's Gospel and John the Baptist invite us to do on the Third

Sunday of Advent. Stand and deliver. Testify to the reality of an undeserved gift that has been given to us.

> Go, tell it on the mountain,
> over the hills and everywhere;
> go, tell it on the mountain,
> that Jesus Christ is born.
> (African American spiritual)

Christians are those who have been surprised by some good news and now are eager to share that news with those who haven't yet heard the news. If you receive some surprisingly good news, you'll find a way to share it.

"Hey, guess what I just saw...."

"You'll never believe what just happened to me...."

How did you get here in church, exploring the mystery of the Incarnation? You are here only because someone "sent from God" told you the truth about Christ. Someone became a witness to you that the Babe born in Bethlehem was the best news you'll ever hear. Somebody had to surprise you, someone like John the Baptist—a witness who pointed your gaze toward the Way, the Truth, and the Light.

Maybe your witness was a beloved grandmother who read Bible stories to you. Perhaps your witness was a fellow student who sat on the side of a bed in a dormitory room in college and argued with you into the night and overcame your sophomoric doubts about the faith. Or maybe your witness was a writer of a book, someone whom you have never met, who said just the right words to you whereby you "saw the light," as we sometimes say. (That's my prayer, in writing this Advent book: "Lord, let me be somebody's witness. Come on, Lord, let your light shine through me, even me. Make me somebody's John the Baptist.")

There's something about this God determined to make connection with humanity, to speak to us through ordinary people like John the Baptist, "sent from God" to witness to the Light. If someone had not been a witness to you, you'd still be in the dark.

In the Acts of the Apostles, Jesus, after being crucified and then raised, meets with the disciples in Jerusalem. They are astounded to see their Lord, who had been so cruelly crucified and buried, back among them, speaking with them, urging them forward beyond their grief. The risen Christ said to those followers, not "You will shortly be joining me in heaven," or "I want you to go out and teach everybody my philosophy of life," or "I need you now to get busy working for peace with justice," though some of that may have been implied.

What Jesus called them was "my witnesses" (Acts 1:8). I'm sending you out, just like my Father sent out a man named John, sending you into all the world to tell the world the truth about me, to hand over the news: Surprise! God is coming into the world as one of us in order to save all of us.

So here's your Advent, Christmas gospel, good news: There was a person sent from God whose name was Amy (or Tom, or Barry, or June, or _____). The witness was nobody special, an average sort of person who was "sent from God." Why sent? "As a witness to testify concerning the light" so that through their witness, "everyone would believe in the light." The witness "wasn't the light," not even close, not even able to tie the sandal straps of the One to whom the witness testified. But for some reason, the Light chose not to shine without the testimony of the witness.

In John's Gospel Jesus majestically pronounces, "I am the light of the world" (John 8:12). Matthew has Jesus turn to this ragtag, uncomprehending, not-always-faithful, timid team of knuckleheaded disciples and say in essence, "You're the light of the world. Shine!" (see Matthew 5:14-16). "This is our message...God is light!" (see 1 John 1:5). What's your chief task as a follower of Jesus? Let Jesus shine on you so that he can then shine in the world through you.

I met a woman who hands a printed card to anyone she meets who might be an undocumented migrant. The card has her name, address, and phone number. She says to them, "If anyone, anywhere, anytime threatens you or someone you love with deportation or incarceration, you call me immediately. I'm not sure what I'm going to do, but Jesus has sent me to stand with you and to speak up for you. Don't be afraid!"

Perhaps the coming year will be a time when many churches will rediscover the boldness and joy of discipleship in an otherwise fearful and depressing time. I know a church that baptized an immigrant family from Afghanistan. Just before the water was poured over their heads, the pastor said, "Church, if we baptize 'em then we've got to protect 'em. God calls us to offer more than friendly hospitality; we've got to promise God long-term generosity and relationship with these whom God has sent to us." Some of the pastor's people said for the first time they understood what baptism is all about.

Think about someone you know, maybe someone at work, or school, or in your own family, who needs some good news, someone who has not yet gotten the message that God is with us. How about inviting that person to join your church as it celebrates Christmas Eve? Christmas Eve is usually church at our best. Why don't you be a witness to the good news by inviting someone to join us as we stand in wonder before the grand mystery of the Incarnation?

Fear not! By God's grace, it's Advent, the beginning of a whole new year. I bring you tidings of great joy. Now, go find somebody who needs to see the Light and tell them all about it.

Chapter

4

Rejoice

CHAPTER 4

Rejoice

When Elizabeth was six months pregnant, God sent the angel Gabriel to Nazareth, a city in Galilee, to a virgin who was engaged to a man named Joseph, a descendant of David's house. The virgin's name was Mary. When the angel came to her, he said, "Rejoice, favored one! The Lord is with you!" She was confused by these words and wondered what kind of greeting this might be. The angel said, "Don't be afraid, Mary. God is honoring you. Look! You will conceive and give birth to a son, and you will name him Jesus. He will be great and he will be called the Son of the Most High. The Lord God will give him the throne of David his father. He will rule over Jacob's house forever, and there will be no end to his kingdom."

Then Mary said to the angel, "How will this happen since I haven't had sexual relations with a man?"

The angel replied, "The Holy Spirit will come over you and the power of the Most High will overshadow you. Therefore, the one who is to be born will be holy. He will be called God's Son. Look, even in her old age, your relative Elizabeth has conceived a son. This woman who was labeled 'unable to conceive' is now six months pregnant. Nothing is impossible for God."

Then Mary said, "I am the Lord's servant. Let it be with me just as you have said." Then the angel left her.

Mary got up and hurried to a city in the Judean highlands. She entered Zechariah's home and greeted Elizabeth. When Elizabeth heard Mary's greeting, the child leaped in her womb, and Elizabeth was filled with the Holy Spirit. With a loud voice she blurted out, "God has blessed you above all women, and he has blessed the child you carry. Why do I have this honor, that the mother of my Lord should come to me? As soon as I heard your greeting, the baby in my womb jumped for joy. Happy is she who believed that the Lord would fulfill the promises he made to her."

Mary said,

> "With all my heart I glorify the Lord!
>> In the depths of who I am I rejoice in God my savior.
> He has looked with favor on the low status of his servant.
>> Look! From now on, everyone will consider me highly favored

because the mighty one has done great
    things for me.
Holy is his name.
    He shows mercy to everyone,
        from one generation to the next,
        who honors him as God.
He has shown strength with his arm.
    He has scattered those with arrogant thoughts
    and proud inclinations.
    He has pulled the powerful down from their
    thrones
        and lifted up the lowly.
He has filled the hungry with good things
    and sent the rich away empty-handed.
He has come to the aid of his servant Israel,
    remembering his mercy,
        just as he promised to our ancestors,
            to Abraham and to Abraham's descendants
            forever."

Mary stayed with Elizabeth about three months, and
then returned to her home.

                                    (Luke 1:26–56)

What a wondrous song is sung as we stand upon the threshold of the Nativity. Even if you don't know much about the Bible, if you know Christmas carols, there's a high probability that you know the words of this song, the story of the angel Gabriel being sent by God to a young woman in an out-of-the-way town in Galilee, telling her that she is a "favored one" of God and that the Lord is with her.

This announcement was made by the angel to Mary "when Elizabeth was six months pregnant." Elizabeth is a relative of Mary. Unlike Mary, she is a very old, childless woman. The angel Gabriel visited her husband, Zechariah, and promised that, even though they were advanced in age, Elizabeth would have a baby. Elizabeth's baby would grow up to be John the Baptist, the preacher whom we heard inaugurate Advent in Mark's Gospel.

I'm all for preaching like that of John the Baptizer, but sometimes our faith is better sung than said. Luke insists that before we can get to Christmas and Jesus's miraculous birth we must first meet a couple of women—neither of whom are preachers, one, a very old woman, Elizabeth, and the other a very young woman, Mary—and listen to them sing. Luke's prelude to Christmas occurs in an obstetrics waiting room that's been transformed into a musical theater.

Mary and Elizabeth are Near Eastern, first-century women. They are vulnerable people on the margins, with few rights. Furthermore, one of the women, Elizabeth, is elderly. She and her husband have no children, which also means that she and her aging husband could have a bleak old age; children were valued as the Near Eastern, first-century equivalent of our Social Security.

Mary is Elizabeth's relative. She is also marginalized and vulnerable—poor, young, but not yet married. An unmarried woman with a baby? How is she going to explain that? People will talk. And yet, Mary responds by saying to the heavenly messenger, "I don't know what this means, but I'm willing to trust God, bear this child, and see where this leads."

INCARNATION

The Old Testament saves apocalyptic until close to the end, with books like Daniel and Ezekiel. Mark gives an apocalyptic speech to Jesus at the end, as he predicts the destruction of the temple. In Luke's Gospel from the get-go, as soon as Mary's opening song, it's new heaven and new earth, world turned upside down, the rise and fall of many, the proud brought low, and the lowly lifted up. Bad news for those of us who are rich, good news for the poor and dispossessed.

Sorry if you prefer your God to keep a respectful distance from the world, to float high above in the realm of ideas, beliefs, and vague, spiritual concepts. Israel's God shows up, comes close, gets all mixed up in our humanity (and in the case of these two women, gynecology). We can't encounter the Son of God, Light of the World, Savior of All without first being engaged by these two human beings, conversing about their utterly human, mundane, obstetric concerns.

In an age when many say, "I'm not religious, but I am very spiritual" (meaning, I've cranked down my religion into vague, inner, ethereal, unthreatening feelings that I keep mostly to myself), the time has never been better to think with Luke's Gospel about Incarnation. "God" is not some notion we have worked up for ourselves. God self-defined by the Incarnation is God coming to us; God deciding to be our God before we decide to be for God, God down and dirty with us, God uncomfortably close.

To one of his sorriest congregations Paul exclaimed, "You are God's temple and God's Spirit lives in you" (1 Corinthians 3:16). It's just what you would expect from a person who had been met by a bodily resurrected, incarnational God on the Damascus road (Acts 9) even though he wasn't out looking for God.

If God could show up to these two otherwise unknown women, God could show up to anybody, anywhere. Even to you, even to me, even here, even now. Incarnation.

Having been met by an embodied God who is active in the bodily, maternal concerns of Mary, who bears Jesus in her womb, we are justified in expecting God to meet us anywhere. Having been reached by the born-in-the-flesh Jew from Nazareth, Jesus, we are more likely to look for God at church and at the soup kitchen. Like the Bethlehem shepherds, we see God in angelic voices in the night sky and at a smelly cow stable. I expect to see something of Jesus in the dear saint at church and in the disagreeable, right-wing politician with whom I debate immigration policy at the statehouse. If God could show up to these two otherwise unknown women, God could show up to anybody, anywhere. Even to you, even to me, even here, even now. Incarnation.

I once asked a medical missionary I knew, "Bob, how did you, Ivy League educated, volunteer for service as a missionary in Africa?"

The surgical resident responded, "I was between surgeries and excused myself into the men's room. As I was standing at the urinal, it was just like the word *Africa* appeared on the wall right before me. I knew what God wanted me to do."

"Bob, don't ever tell that story to anyone who asks how you were called to be a missionary. It makes Jesus look ridiculous," I said, in love.

"It happened just like that," the doctor responded.

"I don't care how it happened, I'm telling you, it's so weirdly incarnational as to make Jesus look ridiculous," said I.

O the antics of an incarnational God!

Where just two or three of us gather, Christ promises to be there (Matthew 18:20). Having shown up to Mary; to Paul; to Matthew, Mark, Luke, Martha, and Dr. Bob, you can count on Jesus to show up to you.

I know, I know. You have been conditioned to think that religion is something you do, a ritual or a good work you perform, some noble thought you work up within yourself, or a high-sounding sentiment you feel. The Incarnation, a gift given to us totally at God's initiative, reassures you that your relationship to God is God's self-assigned task. Even if you don't come to church, that can't keep an incarnational God from coming to you.

When I asked about her eldest son, she replied, "Sadly, my son, who grew up attending Duke Chapel with us, is no longer a Christian. Says he's an atheist."

"He's not a Christian *yet*," I corrected her. "You tell him to keep looking over his shoulder on his way through life. God's got ways."

"They will be my people, and I will be their God," was the divine promise given during one of Israel's most desperate hours (Jeremiah 24:7). That incarnational vow is kept not only throughout scripture but also in your church and mine this coming Sunday, a promise that has particular resonance during Advent. Jeremiah 24:7 is not only a promise but also a command or an invitation, maybe even a warning, depending on how you look at it.

I asked a distinguished new church planter what virtue he most looked for when selecting clergy to be potential church planters. I figured he'd reply with a list of tips and tricks, techniques for surefire new church starts.

"A robust theology of the Incarnation," he replied. "Only someone who believes that God is relentlessly reaching out to save the world has the faith required to birth a new church. If Mary didn't hear that angel right, church planting is impossible."

And the Incarnation wasn't just amazing in that God showed up. It was surprising *to whom* God showed up. Take just a moment and ponder that when God advented among us, when God acted decisively to reach out for us, God came to Elizabeth and Mary. The story of our redemption begins with God bypassing the centers of power, big men at the center, omnipotent, influential men like King Herod up at the palace. The story begins with two women. One of the women, Elizabeth, is a woman in pain because of her childlessness. Being without a child meant, in that day, she is a woman without a future. Without progeny, she has little hope for much of a tomorrow.

Then Gabriel speaks to her husband and Elizabeth becomes pregnant. Elizabeth realizes that the future is up to God and God is graciously giving her a tomorrow that she did not earn for herself. Grace.

The other woman, Mary, is also a powerless person with no special attributes or experiences, so far as Luke tells us. She is unmarried, which means she has no one to protect her.

If you happen to be someone who has been pushed to the margins, silenced by the insensitivity or cruelty of others, told that you don't count because you are not on top or at the center, please pay careful attention to this Advent story.

INCONCEIVABLY CALLED

Once God promised "I will be your God and you will be my people," the direction was cast for human history. First God elects Israel, not because of any positive disposition or talent in Israel, but simply because "God loves you." Chosen not for privilege or power, Israel is given a task: to be a light shining forth to all nations (Isaiah 42:6), a showcase of what God can do once God elects a people and gives them a job to do.

God's determination to be God for the whole world is accomplished by calling a few particular people to be witnesses for God. God starts small—a son is given to old Abraham and Sarah—and expands to a people, Israel; then contracts into a couple of Jewish women in Nazareth; then to a baby born in

Bethlehem; then enlarges to twelve disciples (Luke 6:12-16), then seventy-two (Luke 10:1-24). God's activity explodes from Jerusalem, into Judea, Samaria, and the ends of the earth (Acts 1:8), reaching all the way to your church and mine. A few chosen for the universal good of all. With God, nothing is impossible.

> *When Elizabeth heard Mary's greeting, the child leaped in her womb, and Elizabeth was filled with the Holy Spirit. With a loud voice she blurted out, "God has blessed you above all women, and he has blessed the child you carry."*

The minute Mary shows up at Elizabeth's house, Elizabeth (without any theological training, certification, or public-speaking experience) becomes a prophet. Like the prophets of old, Elizabeth is "filled with the Holy Spirit." Then, prompted by the Holy Spirit, Elizabeth foretells to Mary the significance of Mary's vocation to carry the Son of God into the world. Inspired by the Holy Spirit, Elizabeth even predicts the future work to be done by the child in Mary's womb.

In another Gospel, Jesus says that when ordinary disciples are dragged into court or are facing charges from the authorities, they won't need to come up with the right words to say in their defense. The same Holy Spirit who descended upon Elizabeth, telling her what to say, will give us the speech to deliver, even if we've never been in a seminary homiletics class, or words to that effect (Mark 13:11). Nobody has to be faithful to the Holy Spirit's vocation on their own. God equips with the Holy Spirit those whom God favors by calling them to witness, to preach, to conduct a just and fair hardware business, to form a godly family, to show people how to be environmentally conscious citizens, to run for public office, to raise children who know that they are God's, to do work that others may think they are too good to do, or to prophesy about the future.

To the few from the margins whom God calls to lead the revolution, God says, "I'm going to take back my beloved but wayward creation. Guess who's going to help me?"

> *When the angel came to her, he said, "Rejoice, favored one! The Lord is with you!" She was confused by these words and wondered what kind of greeting this might be. The angel said, "Don't be afraid, Mary. God is honoring you. Look! You will conceive and give birth to a son, and you will name him Jesus....Then Mary said to the angel, "How will this happen ...?*

Mary realizes that she is somebody, blessed, fortunate, given a job to do in the salvation of the world. Even in her youth and singleness, her embarrassment and consternation, she is called. She is singled out by God to bear the Savior of the world into the world. That's why the church has often called Mary "the first disciple." She is the first to be called by God to take a part in the good newsing of the world. And she is the first, when called by God, to say, "Yes. Here I am. Send me."

Mary was honored by the church for her docile submission to God's inscrutable will. I praise her for her courageous determination and wild willingness to be jolted by the promises of God and say, "God only knows where all this is headed, but count me in."

(By the way: I don't think this story of Mary and her pregnancy is told by Luke to make a statement about the ethics of abortion. Still, if you are dealing with an embarrassing, hard-to-explain, difficult pregnancy, Mary's story does give you pause.)

"Have you always enjoyed working with the homeless?" I asked him. I knew him to be an attorney, a member of one of our most affluent congregations. Yet there he was, washing breakfast dishes at 6:30 in the morning at an inner-city church by, for, and with the homeless.

"Who told you I enjoyed working with the homeless?" he asked with a smirk. "You ever had a conversation with any of these guys? They're in a mess. One of 'em broke into my car yesterday when I was in here washing his dirty dishes!"

"But er…uh, there you are, at this hour of the morning. How did you decide to be part of this ministry?" I persisted.

"I didn't get to decide," the lawyer responded. "Jesus insisted. Put me here whether I liked it or not. Let me ask you; how did *you* decide to be a bishop in Alabama? Did you beg to be here?"

Such is God's rambunctious call.

Mary's initial response to Gabriel's words is doubt, pondering, and wonderment. Who wouldn't respond this way? Mary has multiple reasons to be bewildered. Perhaps Mary is flustered and confused because she is shocked to have been the "favored one" of God. Me? I'm a nobody. How is it possible for me to be favored? How could the mighty Lord of Israel enlist and employ somebody as limited as I?

Gabriel then tells her the big news that she's going to be pregnant with a son, but not just any son, the Son of the Most

High, no less, a "king" from the lineage of David, a sovereign with a never-ending reign.

No wonder Mary's initial response is "Are you kidding me?"

Mary said to the angel, "How will this happen...?"

The angel replied, "The Holy Spirit will come over you and the power of the Most High will overshadow you. Therefore, the one who is to be born will be holy. He will be called God's Son. Look, even in her old age, your relative Elizabeth has conceived a son....Nothing is impossible for God."

In Mary, a story of God's advent and promise keeping becomes a story of human acceptance of God's vocation.

Even in her bewilderment, Mary moves from a confused "How can this be?" to the embracing, "Let it be with me just as you have said." God really is making good on God's promises (Luke 1:36). That grand shift from disbelief to "Here I am" is quite a move in just a couple of verses. In Mary, a story of God's advent and promise keeping becomes a story of human acceptance of God's vocation. No wonder that Mary has always been regarded by the church as the premier disciple, the first to be enlisted by God to play a role in the Jesus story who gives a model discipleship response, "I don't fully understand why you favored me with such a vocation, but here I am."

I hope that you hear this story of God coming first to these two otherwise unknown, lowly women on the margins—one who is young and the other who is old—as maybe your story. Let's face it, most of us are unknown to the world. We are living in a place that's nice enough, but our neighborhood is not that of the prestigious and prominent. To none of us has been given the power to run the world.

And Luke's Gospel says, Rejoice! You are just the sort of person, young or old, to whom God might turn and enlist to play your part in God's great revolutionary, reclamation, redemption project in the world.

Don't believe Luke? You doubt that it's possible for God to come to you like God turned to Mary and Elizabeth? Please listen to the angel: "Nothing is impossible for God."

CALLED TO BE PART
OF A REVOLUTION

The song that Mary sings is no sweet lullaby; it's a clench-fisted battle cry. In Mary's song, we begin to hear truth about the revolution that Jesus brings to the world. God has favored one of "low status" to fire the opening salvo. God has not only blessed her, a lowly person, but through her God has favored all the poor and the lowly. God has taken sides. God not only blesses the poor and the hungry but curses the rich and the powerful. Those on the bottom are being lifted up;

those at the top are being pushed down. In this birth a great, God-wrought reversal is taking place.

The change that God intends is bigger than a change of hearts. It's more than personal; it's systemic transformation, cosmic shaking of heaven and earth:

> *"He has shown strength with his arm.*
>> *He has scattered those with arrogant thoughts and proud inclinations.*
>> *He has pulled the powerful down from their thrones and lifted up the lowly.*
> *He has filled the hungry with good things and sent the rich away empty-handed.*
> *He has come to the aid of his servant Israel, remembering his mercy, just as he promised to our ancestors, to Abraham and to Abraham's descendants forever."*
>
> *(Luke 1:51-55)*

Well, you said you wanted God to come down and do something. Who knew God's advent would be this disruptive? Mary's song is good news for some, bad news for others. Much depends on the salary you're making and the car you're driving when you get the news. It's curious that Mary sings in the past tense. In using the past tense ("He has…"), Mary claims that the great reversal of lifting up the lowly and casting down the powerful and proud is already in motion and has been for some time.

No need to pray for God to show up and begin to act like God. From the beginning, God was for us, even though we had not the sense to see it. God has always been clear that God was on the side of widows, orphans, the hungry, the homeless, victims, and sufferers. Who God is and what God wants is an accomplished fact. Read the Bible. Wake up. Face facts, open your eyes. Emmanuel is not just a name for God's Son, it's a description of what God was doing all through the ages.

One more time now, everybody singing the chorus:

> *He has filled the hungry with good things*
> *and sent the rich away empty-handed.*
> *He has come to the aid of his servant Israel.*

The Incarnation is not God's last act of desperation when everything else God tried before didn't work. After so many centuries of failure, God said in exasperation, "I've got an idea! I'll take on human flesh and be born of a virgin! Maybe that will finally grab their attention!"

No. By singing her song in the past tense ("He has…"), Mary implies that God was not performing some surprising new work that is out of character for God. God didn't start being our salvation with the advent of Jesus. God didn't suddenly turn from the rich toward the poor. Scripture recounts a long series of divine interventions whereby God blesses those in need and judges the powerful and the mighty. Remember the Exodus? Israel's God went head-to-head with mighty Pharaoh to liberate the enslaved. Recall Israel's prophets who spoke out and acted up in front of powerful kings. That's the same God who impregnated Mary.

Here on the eve of Christmas, the angel comes to Mary and says, "Rejoice, favored one! The Lord is with you!" All heaven is breaking loose. God's revolution has begun.

He pompously pronounced, "I wouldn't be part of any church that teaches that racism is systemic, that there's something wrong with the American way. Nor do I tolerate any 'woke' talk about 'social justice' or 'systemic change.'"

When I asked him if he attended any church, he said, "Yep, I'm a Catholic."

"Really?" I responded in amazement. "Aren't you guys big on the Virgin Mary? Have you ever heard her sing?"

We are told nothing about the background or qualifications of Mary or Elizabeth. Perhaps this is Luke's way of underscoring that this is not primarily a story about two courageous women who stepped up and heroically witnessed to and became part of God's revolutionary take back of God's world. The most interesting actor in this drama is God.

Two ordinary, previously unknown people are summoned, commissioned, pushed out onto the stage, and given roles to play in the world's revolutionary redemption by a God who delights in that sort of thing. No doubt, these two women are extraordinary in saying, "Don't know why you are calling me, but I'll say yes and see where all this leads." But most astonishing of all in this Advent story is a God who acts in history by summoning, commissioning, and pushing out on stage ordinary folk like Elizabeth and Mary, giving them a job to do for God.

While Mary is right to sing that it is a blessed thing to be favored by God to do some important task, Mary is also right in saying that God's call can be inconceivable (no pun intended). *Why me? Why not commandeer somebody else's life? I don't have the skill set to accomplish this task. The timing is not right. Give me a chance to get past my health problems and then I'll be open to your proposition. I tend to vote conservative. I've already got enough on my plate at the moment. This doesn't fit my life plan. Let me pray about it awhile and get back to you.* Those are frequent first responses from disciples who sense God's call upon their lives.

And yet, whatever it is that God wants to do to shake up God's world, God has chosen to do it not without the assistance of ordinary folk like Mary, Elizabeth, Joe, Sophie, and maybe even you.

Timing not good for you? Unmarried? Immature? Too old? Too young? Lack the education and preparation? Got too much education? Pregnant? Not good at public speaking? Afraid of conflict? Nervous and unsteady? Unskilled at the suppression of the rich and the uplifting of the poor? God doesn't care; God will call you anyway.

Mary and Elizabeth could tell you all about it.

FROM THE MARGINS

Sure, it's a blessing to have God advent among us. But it is important to note that Luke's telling the stories of these two women and their singing and prophesying makes some very specific claims about the favor and the blessing of God. God comes to this unmarried, young, powerless peasant woman in an out-of-the-way little town. God favors an older, childless woman, Elizabeth. What does that tell you about God?

> *God sent the angel Gabriel to Nazareth, a city in Galilee, to a virgin who was engaged to a man named Joseph, a descendant of David's house. The virgin's name was Mary....Mary got up and hurried to a city in the Judean highlands. She entered Zechariah's home and greeted Elizabeth.*

Judea is nobody's idea of the center of the universe. And Nazareth is the outback of Judea. I've been to Nazareth, walked its dusty streets, stayed in one of its rundown hotels, been subjected to the cries of street vendors hawking their wares, and jostled by herds of tourists stumbling off buses that belched diesel fumes.

"What a place for God Almighty to show up," I muttered to myself.

I've been to occupied, conflicted, powder keg Bethlehem. I've seen the wall separating Palestinians and Israelis and the soldiers armed to the teeth, witnessed Christians squabbling with one another over just whose turf is the Church of the Nativity.

"What a location for the birth of Emmanuel," I smirked.

Be honest. Most of us live in places that are unknown to the rest of the world. Sure, our location is named Durham, Des Moines, Duluth, or Dallas; but during Advent, we all live in Nazareth. Bethlehem. Mary's song reminds us that our social, geographic, economic remoteness doesn't stump God's vocational intent. God surprised Mary and Elizabeth by showing up where they were and making things happen in them in order to make good things occur in the world. It's Advent. Be careful to whom you open your door.

I was minding my own business trying to be a teenager in Greenville, South Carolina (ever heard of it?), when God showed up to me (had you heard of me before you bought this book?) and, even though I had not the proper personality configuration and lacked any ministerial credentials, God called me to be a preacher. True, my vocation was not as dramatic or embarrassing as someone like Mary being impregnated by the Holy Spirit, still.... I think it is important for you to know that writing this book wasn't my idea.

NOTHING IMPOSSIBLE

Everything turns on Gabriel's pronouncement, "Nothing is impossible for God" (Luke 1:37). The virgin conception of Jesus is only the beginning of God's surprises. Wait until you see what happens after Jesus's death. Nothing is off the table. Nothing impossible.

"My son is addicted to cocaine. You think it's possible for him ever to be clean?" she asked. From what I hear, the instances of those who survive such addiction are few. No. Your son is trapped, doomed by the impossible. No tomorrow for you.

"It's impossible for us to find the money to do the repairs needed to keep the church day care center open." Increasing numbers of churches are finding it hard to make ends meet. End of the line for the mainline. Future, impossible.

116

"If you think it's possible to revive this dwindling congregation, you are deluding yourself," said the church growth consultant. Get real. Face facts. Give up. Impossible.

So many of the problems that we face seem intractable. *Unless Gabriel's words are true.* With us, impossible. But with the God who was implicated in the pregnancies of two women, one young and unmarried, one old and without a future, well, maybe the impossible could be possible.

When the sky is dark, when our roads come to a dead end, or we run into a brick wall, when time has run out and there's no tomorrow, that's when the God of Mary and Elizabeth loves to advent, show up, and take time for us, making our time God's time.

Thank God, God did not wait until all the world was ready, until we had exhausted our attempts to be gods unto ourselves and were desperate for relief. Nor did God wait until we had figured out that it just makes sense for us frail, finite creatures to be in loving connection with our Creator.

God did not delay until we were finally at peace, and all the fretful nations were at one accord, hands joined in universal comity. No conditions were put on God's coming to us, no waiting until we had at last come to our senses and lived up to our great human potential, by following our better angels and doing what was right.

When God took time for us, the sky was dark, the future unsteady and threatening, prisoners languished in their cells and cried out for release, and the poor were at their wits' end due to oppression by the rich. Tyrants raged unchecked. Kingdoms propped themselves up with big armies and the news was mostly bad.

Thank God that God didn't wait for the perfect time but came when the times were out of joint and our need was great. We had lost faith in so many of our leaders, institutions, and traditions and had proven so many times that we couldn't help ourselves by ourselves.

Thank God that God didn't wait for the perfect time but came when the times were out of joint and our need was great.

"When the fulfillment of the time came" (Galatians 4:4), when God showed up, Son of the Father, Emmanuel, God with us, God Almighty stooping, dining with sinners, undeterred by the grime they brought to the table, God ignored politicians and their ilk. God didn't wait until we had gotten our lives together. Thank God, God came anyway.

To the anguish and trauma and pain, all of it, Christ came and did not flinch from sharing our full, human lot. Christ paid a high price (the cross) for turning to us in our time, becoming one of us, but Christ came anyway.

Christ came as Light and, no matter how hard we tried, we couldn't extinguish the Light of the World. It shined, still shines anyway.

Christ came into our world as it is, but refused to leave it as it was. While Christ embraced our world, Christ refused to mesh with it, telling us the truth, refusing to respect our traditions and institutions, risking offense, never backing down from an argument with those who thought they knew everything about God, turning over the tables on us and our placid, compromised religion.

So here's some good news with your name on it: Christ does not wait until you've got your life all together and are at a good place, comfortable in your skin, at peace with yourself and all around you, sure in your convictions, steady in your faith, all cleaned up and shiny, prepared for Advent. He comes anyway, because that's who Christ is.

Christ came as a babe, a vulnerable little child, born into a poor family, in an out-of-the-way sort of place, unheralded by the powerful and the well-heeled, welcomed only by a few shepherds, some magicians from the East, and an embarrassed couple from Nazareth.

We who have witnessed this wonder, let us not wait until the world is at peace to announce God's peace. Let's not keep to ourselves the news we've heard sung. Let's refuse to be constrained by what the world thinks is possible or intimidated by what the world tells us to be impossible. Our humanity, in all its flaws and weakness, failures and cruelty, has been embraced. Let's not wait to sing.

GOOD NEWS

"The Lord is with you!" Good news or bad? Confused Mary wondered "what kind of greeting this might be."

I've got a friend who characterizes (I hope, in jest) my preaching as "six reasons you're not really a Christian even though you may have thought you were when you came to church this Sunday." Church is where you come to find out all the ways you fail to be good at being a member of the church. Preachers are those who enumerate how you are not as adept at Christian discipleship as the preacher.

I heard the dean of a medical school say (surely tongue-in-cheek), "A well person is merely a patient on whom we need to run a few more tests." A doctor is one who tells you that you're sicker than you thought.

"Why do you no longer attend church?" I asked a lapsed Christian.

"Because I got tired of being beaten up every Sunday and being told what's wrong with me, my country, and my world. I quit because I never heard any good news that I didn't know, that was better than all the bad news that everybody already knows."

When church loses sight of a God who forgives, a God who makes a revolutionary way when there is no way, a Savior who relentlessly seeks and saves sinners, church gets ugly. Sunday morning becomes a long session with your high school Latin teacher who hands you a paper defaced by red marks that prove you can't possibly be smart enough or work hard enough to learn Latin.

"Why is the average age of my congregation sixty-five? Because these self-centered, lazy millennials just aren't as religious as their parents," pontificated the boomer preacher.

Surprise, no millennials have been attracted by this preacher's sermons.

Scolding sermons pervert the good news (gospel) of Jesus Christ into the bad news of all that you simply must do to chin up to God, an inventory of the myriad ways you've failed to measure up to God's expectations.

In my church family, sermonic dressing-down (often labeled as "prophetic preaching") goes something like "This week, church, I want you to work on your sexism, racism, classism, and ageism. Come back next Sunday and I'll give you a new list." Few hearts rise upon hearing such scolding. This type of preaching is pathetic rather than prophetic.

A few years ago I saw a list of things you can do to improve your mental health. Top of the list was "refuse to watch the local news."

There is no news on the TV evening news except bad news. When they attempt a bit of good news, say in the last four minutes of the news program, it's always some sappy story of a lost kitty cat rescued from a tree, or a puppy who found his way back home ("See, we are nicer people than is indicated by this program's previous reports of human mayhem and cruelty."), good news so trivial that it's hardly an antidote to all the bad news.

If you manage to avoid depressingly bad news Monday through Saturday, and show up in church on a Sunday, I'll deliver in my sermon the bad news about you that you've overlooked. On and on with the bad news.

The bad news is so depressing because what's wrong with you and the things that are messed up about your world are mostly out of your control. If it were in your power fully to follow my three quick-and-easy steps (enunciated in my self-help sermon "Three Steps to a Better You"), you would have done so already.

"CONNECT WITH JOY!" proclaims a billboard outside of town, paid for by my denomination. It seems to be part of an expensive advertising campaign to attract folks to The United Methodist Church. True, Advent is about joy, but it's not joy that we receive by coming to our senses, showing up at church, and connecting with God to get our jolt of joy.

Ask people "What is the gospel?" and many reply "I must believe that Jesus died for my sins so that when I die my soul can go to heaven." Jesus becomes the passive automaton who was briefly among us, who trudged directly to his death, thereby winning our ticket to eternity, provided we believe the right beliefs about Jesus. Too much is left out: Jesus's life is detached from Jesus's death, Christ merely sets a bar and sits back to see if you can live up to it. Christ lives, dies, and leaves. Too much is left up to us: our salvation is conditional upon our thinking, believing, and deciding.

Christ's salvation becomes your personal quiz that, if passed, leads to the optimum individual eternal destination. Your believing becomes the condition of your salvation. Close your eyes and try hard to believe this and God will give you that. This, good news? No joy in that.

Say you are one of those people who worry deeply about climate change and the way we have despoiled the earth and poisoned our air and water. Good for you. The scientists urge us to act now. Do as I do: install solar panels on your roof, eat less red meat, don't use plastic bags, recycle, compost, and pedal faster. But then we hear that half of the scientists say we've already waited too late to do much about it.

Alas, doing your bit isn't enough to impact the climate catastrophe that looms before us. Once again, too little, too late.

It's depressing.

Maybe so many preachers preach bad news because it's so readily available without the intervention of the Holy Spirit. Just search "climate crisis" or "Ukraine" on the web and you'll harvest enough bad news to tide you over until the next calamity if we make it that far. You don't need to ponder scripture or read a book like this to hear bad news. Bad news is low-hanging fruit for a preacher.

Good news can only come as a divine gift. Though your sin is so obvious that any lazy preacher can get sermons from CNN or Fox, good news, gospel, is to be had only through scripture and the empowering of the Holy Spirit.

So, there you are at church on the Fourth Sunday of Advent, expecting to be beat over the head for your sin. Then we open up the scriptures and to our surprise find that, though there's lots of bad news to be confronted, and our sin is ubiquitous and obvious, all three of this Sunday's Advent lessons will have none of it. Merry Christmas. The news this day is all good. Your sin doesn't stump God.

And though it might be tempting for me to point to evidence of some of your weaknesses, bad habits, wrong ideas, and lousy attitudes, the scripture's word on the last Sunday of Advent won't let me. It's a song of pure, unrestrained, full-throated, robust joy.

Enough already of your sad songs or mournful lament and my sermonic scolding. At the end of Advent, God's people gather to sing Christmas carols and rejoice.

What's the source of our joy? Have we turned off the news, learned to ignore unpleasant facts, put on rose-colored glasses, pasted a goofy smile on our faces, and managed to stop thinking about the climate crisis? Have we taken a mood-enhancing pill?

No. The joy this day is not of our devising. It is joy that is not self-derived or achieved with chemical help. It does not arise from us but rather comes to us. Glad tidings rather than bad chiding or moralistic deriding. The joy that makes us sing—in spite of any other sad or depressing news to the contrary—is the joy that arises when we receive good news of who God is, what God's up to, and with whom.

The joy this day is not of our devising.

If you get good news—say a phone call that tells you that the hospital test shows that you are cancer-free, or that your daughter has just passed her big exam, or that the boss has given you a raise, or that your son is at last delivered of his addiction—nobody must exhort "Rejoice!"

Let me venture, in one long sentence, the good news: God Almighty, the one who created the earth that we despoiled, the good Creator who created humanity only to have humanity, time and again, turn against God—this God has advented, turned toward us, taken time for us, become one of us in order to do something about the problem of us. Rejoice!

How hard we tried to climb up to God, to heft ourselves out of our hemmed-in humanity, to clamber up to the divine. Good news: though we could never get up to God, God has climbed down to us. Rejoice!

Titus, usually read on Christmas, sets the proper laudatory tone: "The grace of God has appeared, bringing salvation to all people" (Titus 2:11). God has not just loved us, God has shown up. God Almighty has refused to stay obscure, relegated to heaven above, tucked safely into eternity. God has appeared among us: "He gave himself for us in order to rescue us" (Titus 2:14). Our most earnest prayers have been heard—God with all of us. Rejoice!

Jesus wants more than a "personal relationship" with you. Jesus is Lord, satisfied with nothing less than being light for the whole darkened world. The good news we've heard in Jesus Christ is good news for all. Therefore our gospel word to the world is not one of recrimination, condemnation, and judgment. Here's not a tune that's meant to be hummed to yourself in the shower; it's a song to be belted out so that it wakes up the whole neighborhood. It's a word that calls upon the whole, fallen, suffering, hurting, fearful world: "Rejoice!"

It's sad when church becomes a place where we merely point to all the evidence that we need saving rather than a place joyfully to celebrate that we are saved. It's sad when people hear the word *church* and think of a place where you go to be told everything that's wrong with you and your world rather than a people who celebrate how God has made things right between us, our world, and God.

SING FOR JOY

Luke confronts a church that's so often stuck in introverted lament by beginning his Gospel with full-throated, raucous singing. Maybe there were believers in Luke's church who had grown tired of waiting for Christ's Second Advent and who therefore needed to be reminded of how much Christ had already accomplished in his first. So Luke presents heavenly angels singing, whose songs were heard all the way down here on earth. Old Zechariah joyfully sings, even though he had long before aged out of the choir. After visiting her childless relative, Elizabeth, Mary bursts into song even though many would question what on earth she had to sing about.

The song that Mary sings is not original with Mary. Her song is closely connected with the song of Hannah back in 1 Samuel 2. Mary's and Hannah's song has been sung by Israel time and again when God's people needed God's intervention and deliverance in the worst sort of way. As strange and unexpected as the pregnancies of Elizabeth and Mary are, God had acted in a similar way before, visiting aging, childless couples, or unmarried, embarrassed couples, and giving them children. A strange and wonderful pregnancy began Israel as a people (remember old Abraham and Sarah?).

When you give someone something that they wanted but never thought they would receive, you'll get a song, even if they are not a gifted singer. Tell someone who thought they were at a dead end that God has made a way when they thought there was no way, they'll sing.

"A B+ !" I heard a student exclaim in a booming voice just outside my office. "And I thought I'd flunked the exam!" I opened my office door and watched him dance down the hallway singing, "Oh, what a beautiful morning! Oh, what a beautiful day."

Joy is a responsive, reflexive emotion. The joyfulness of the song tends to be in proportion to the surprise of the gift and the unlikelihood of receiving the gift.

Mary (a woman, young and unmarried, three strikes against her), Elizabeth (a woman, old, childless) had thought there was no way, no tomorrow.

Surprise! God gives babies, a future, makes a way. And thus they sing.

Hearing such gospel singing, the world harrumphs, "What's there to sing about?"

While I was on a mission trip to staff a medical clinic in Haiti, the poorest country in the Western Hemisphere, I found one of our nurses weeping outside the examination room.

"Are you okay?" I asked. "Anything I can do?"

She replied, "You can tell me why they're singing."

What?

"On and off, all day long, I hear the children at the school. Singing! Most of them will be dead, victims of disease or hunger, before they can reach twenty-one. What have they got to be singing about? It's the constant Haitian singing that I find hardest to understand."

Hard to understand, yes. And a rebuke to our often-doleful practice of the faith. What enables a hurting world, sometimes those who have been hurt the most, to sing? If they sing, it's probably not as self-congratulation for their personal achievements. There is no adequate psychological, economic, sociological explanation for the song. It must be theological; what Mary and Elizabeth sing of God is true. Gabriel was right; with God nothing is impossible. And that's why you'll hear Christmas carols being sung by those who, without God, would have nothing.

I knew a preacher who vainly attempted to mount an argument for the virginal conception of Jesus in his Christmas Eve sermon. The miracle of Incarnation can make sense to you, he claimed, if you just think about it in the right way. I'll tell you how.

To the man's credit, fortunately, he realized what an impossible task he had set for himself in the sermon. Sixteen minutes into his sputtering proofs, reasons, and rationales he stopped himself midsentence and blurted out, "To heck with it. This kind of truth is better sung. Let's all stand and sing "Joy to the World."

Good for him.

My friend the rabbi grumbled, "Hanukkah is a lame holiday compared with Christmas. It's never been an important religious holiday in Judaism and never will be. Besides, you Christians have all the good songs. 'Dreidel, Dreidel, Dreidel' can't compete with 'O Little Town of Bethlehem.'" Joyful Christmas carols, just what you'd expect from people who believe that God became the baby in Mary's womb and moved in with us.

> Peace on earth, and mercy mild,
> God and sinners reconciled!
> (Charles Wesley, "Hark the Herald Angels Sing")

God is not distant, aloof, high and lifted up. God is a babe in a manger, the light shining into our darkness. When we sing those joyful words in Handel's *Messiah,* inspired from Isaiah 9:6, "For unto us a child is born, unto us a son is given," we celebrate that God located, became specific and self-defined, unveiled, revealed in Jesus, the "newborn baby wrapped snugly and lying in a manger" (Luke 2:12).

Isaiah announces the light that shines on "the people walking in darkness" (Isaiah 9:2). God has not left us to stumble along as best we can. God loves us enough to come alongside and to do something decisive about the problem between us and God. Any God who would dare to impregnate a young virgin woman and somehow assist in the impregnation of an old, childless woman must be the sort of outrageous God who will stoop to anything in order to outrageously be God for us rather than God aloof from us.

One of the challenges I faced as Dean of Duke University Chapel was Christmas Eve. From a layperson's point of view, Christmas Eve was the best time to be at Duke Chapel—with the magnificent Gothic chapel fully decorated, twinkling in candlelight, hosting three jam-packed evening services. Yet from a preacher's point of view, Christmas Eve at the chapel was almost too much.

"They know not why they are here," I said to myself as I watched people fighting to get in for the first service, acting as if they were at a Black Friday sale and not at a church on Christmas Eve. Two thousand people from all over the world, some having traveled hours to be there, stood in line for almost as long, and then, once we opened the doors, pushing, shoving, and scrambling for seats. There were screaming babies, and people young and old who obviously had not been in a service of Christian worship in a long time, if ever.

"Would you like a more suitable location to change that diaper?" I heard an usher ask a father who was attending to his toddler—on the second pew from the front.

"Come all the way from Bunnlevel, tonight better be good," said one, in a threatening voice.

"No donkey this year? Didn't the previous preacher hire a donkey to bring in Mary and the baby Jesus? You've changed so many things we loved about Duke Chapel. Why can't we have a donkey?" whined another, plaintively.

"We do not allow smoking in the building!" I shout to a man lighting a cigar just as a chorister begins "Once in David's Royal City."

Why such throngs, why such eagerness to get into church for a once-a-year visit? Of course, the beauty of the building has something to do with it, and the sentimentality that oozes from everywhere at the yuletide. Yes. But such explanations never adequately explain the eager throngs at Christmas Eve in Duke Chapel.

Here's what I think: though these masses surging in for the Eve of the Nativity may be able to sing along with "O Little Town of Bethlehem," they know next to nothing about Christian theology, certainly nothing of the Christian doctrine of the Incarnation. They don't know Elizabeth or Mary from the unmarried mother at school or the sweet old lady down the street. Yet they do know enough to know that here is celebration of good news *that is good news for them.*

Most of the time the church seems aloof from their lives and unaware of their need. The Christian faith appears complicated, judgmental, and arcane. God? A vague, remote enigma.

But tonight, when a young lector pronounces "The Word was made flesh and dwelt among us," they inchoately but deeply understand that this is a word from God to them. Though they couldn't describe it if they had to, they somehow, deep within themselves, know the truth about God. The carols that they sing so heartily, they know "by heart." God is for us. Love moves the world, all the way down. In the end, Light. Our destiny is communion rather than oblivion. In the beginning and at the end, Jesus Christ, God with us.

That's why they flock in on Christmas Eve. And they sing and tears come to their eyes, even if they can't fully say why, as they are moved to the depths of their souls by the wonder of Incarnation. A miracle that's too big for them to grasp has grasped them.

Christ's saving work—begun in a cow shed in Bethlehem, manifested in Christ's compassionate signs and wonders, endured through the hell of Calvary, continued here and now by Christ's glorious resurrection—is brought to consummation. Creation restored, heaven and earth mingled in indissoluble union, God with us so that we might be with God. Rejoice!

So, lay aside this book and pick up a hymnbook. Get on to the serious business of Christmastide—your joyful singing. There will be other sermons and Sundays when you are given a tough assignment by Jesus like loving your enemies or praying for those who persecute you. Here, at the end of Advent and the beginning of Christmas, it's different. You are given a gracious invitation: Rejoice!

Get on to the serious business of Christmastide—your joyful singing.

Merry Christmas. What the angel said to the shepherds I say to you so that you may go forth and merrily sing it to all, "Rejoice! For unto you is born this day in the city of David, a Savior—Christ the Lord." Rejoice!

WILL WILLIMON

Heaven and Earth: Advent and the Incarnation is the latest of the dozens of Abingdon books that Will has written for the church. Will preaches nearly every Sunday in churches around the world. He is director of the Doctor of Ministry Program at Duke Divinity School where he serves as professor of the practice of Christian ministry. For twenty years he was Dean of the Chapel at Duke University and he has served as bishop in The United Methodist Church.

There are videos and a leader guide to accompany *Heaven and Earth: Advent and the Incarnation.*

Will thanks his two former students, Cameron Merrill and Carter Rief, for their help in editing.

WATCH VIDEOS
BASED ON
HEAVEN AND EARTH:
ADVENT AND THE
INCARNATION
WITH WILL WILLIMON
THROUGH AMPLIFY MEDIA.

Amplify Media is a multimedia platform that delivers high quality, searchable content with an emphasis on Wesleyan perspectives for churchwide, group, or individual use on any device at any time. In a world of sometimes overwhelming choices, Amplify gives church leaders and congregants media capabilities that are contemporary, relevant, effective and, most importantly, affordable and sustainable.

With *Amplify Media* church leaders can:

* Provide a reliable source of Christian content through a Wesleyan lens for teaching, training, and inspiration in a customizable library
* Deliver their own preaching and worship content in a way the congregation knows and appreciates
* Build the church's capacity to innovate with engaging content and accessible technology
* Equip the congregation to better understand the Bible and its application
* Deepen discipleship beyond the church walls

Λ **AMPLIFY** MEDIΛ

Ask your group leader or pastor about Amplify Media and sign up today at www.AmplifyMedia.com.